ALL TIME GREAT BLOOPERS

KERMIT SCHAFER'S

ALL TIME GREAT BLOOPERS

Drawings by Doug Anderson

AVENEL BOOKS · NEW YORK

ISBN: 0-517-132044
Copyright © MCMLXXIII by Blooper Enterprises, Inc.,
a division of Kermit Schafer Productions
Library Of Congress Catalog Card Number: 73-91954
All rights reserved.
This edition is published by Avenel Books
a division of Crown Publishers, Inc.
a b c d e f g h
Manufactured in the United States Of America

DEDICATION

This book is dedicated as a sympathetic tribute to members of the broadcasting industry who have been the victims of Bloopers, in the hope that it offers consolation and proof of the fact that they are not alone.

To err is human,
To forgive, divine.

Alexander Pope

To forgive is human,
To err, divine.

Kermit Schafer

ALL TIME GREAT BLOOPERS

Cutting Remark

Adlai Stevenson, one of America's great statesmen, was known for his remarkable vocabulary. However, even one as great as he was can fall victim to a prize Blooper. The following occurred during a speech that was broadcast nation-wide: "Protest demonstrations have taken place by workers whose trade union rights have been betrayed, by Catholics whose freedom of expression has been circumcized . . . circumscribed." (AUDIENCE LAUGHTER) He then tried to recover with, "Well, I believe it at least is a Christian right."

Air Time

DISK JOCKEY: "And now some lovely songs from Josh Logan's 'Fanny' ".

For the Man Who Has Everything

One of the prizes on the show, "Gambit," was a riding power mower with optional grass catcher. However, the announcer informed the audience that it was "a beautiful riding mower with optional ass scratcher."

Fed Up
Hugh Downs, doing an Alpo dog food commercial on the Today Show, was frustrated by a St. Bernard who was supposed to eat the food with relish during a live commercial. All the dog did, however, was sniff at the bowl and pant into the mike. The exasperated Downs pleaded, "Would you mind explaining why you won't eat?"

For Better or Worse
SPORTSCASTER: Jack Kachave, with a bad knee, limps back to the huddle. He wants to play this game in the worst way . . . and that's exactly what he is doing!

Paging Miss Keeler
The following was heard on the BBC: "I cannot speak for other women, but I have always found that Prime Minister MacMillan satisfied me personally . . . that is, more than any other Cabinet member."

Booze Is the Only Answer
NEWSCASTER: The committee for the charity bazaar starting next Sunday at the Methodist Church has assured us that there will be plenty of booze selling . . . I don't mean booze . . . I mean that there will be plenty of booths selling.

Sing, You Sinners
ANNOUNCER: Our midnight movie tonight features Gene Kelly, Donald O'Connor and Debbie Reynolds in the tuneful 'Sinnin In The Rain' . . . er . . . 'Singing In The Rain.'

Fibber McGee
Newsman Frank McGee, sitting in on The Today Show on NBC-TV, told of ". . . heavy clouds in the wethermost . . . *westernmost* portions and heavy snurf . . . *surf* . . . along the coast!"

He Doesn't Give a Hoot
One night Johnny Carson had an animal trainer as a guest on his Tonight Show. When they had to break for a commercial, Carson advised listeners to: "stay tuned, because right after this we're going to be seeing a horny owl."

Death Takes a Holiday

An announcer at KERV, Kerrville, Texas, read this unnerving bit of information on his "obituary column of the air":

"Karl Smith, 83, a lifetime resident of this city, passed away at his home Tuesday night. Funeral services for Mr. Smith will be held in the chapel of the First Methodist Church. Entertainment will follow in the cemetery. Excuse me, that should have been *interment*."

It's About Time

The early-morning newscaster was apparently not quite awake yet, but he sure woke his listeners up with this agricultural news:

"The farmers in the Annapolis Valley are pleased to announce that this year there will be an abundance of apples. This is particularly good news, because most of the farmers haven't had a good crap in years."

I'd Rather Fight Than Switch

Heard on a Michigan TV station: "Stay tuned for tonight's movie, 'Take the High Ground,' starring Richard Widmark. This is the story of a tough marine sergeant who takes a platoon of fighting men and turns them into a bunch of raw recruits."

Animal Crackers

When Mike Douglas was interviewing Wayne Newton's Japanese wife, they talked about Wayne's love of animals. Mike asked Mrs. Newton, "Have you always liked animals?" "No, not until I met Wayne."

On the Carpet

A KEWI announcer, doing a commercial during the play-by-play coverage of a baseball game, looked up and saw that a batter was at the plate and the next inning was about to start. As a result, he hurried through the end of the commercial, and it came out like this: "If you buy your wall-to-wall carpeting at Ed Marling's this week, Marlings *crapet fartsmen* will install it absolutely free."

Who's On First

During a press conference Senator J. William Fulbright gave the following memorable answer to a reporter's question: "As I said already, they have conducted themselves in the last two or three years, much more discri . . . er, discree . . . discri . . . uh, with greater prudence and discretion than we have, because it is, uh, I . . . I've forgotten what the question was."

Forget Me Not

Heard on WIOD in Miami, Florida: "This is Alan Courtney speaking. Don't forget, tonight at nine, our special guest . . . (PAUSE) . . . will be . . . I forgot."

Give him the Bird

Telephone talk shows on radio are particularly good sources of Bloopers. When Art Merrill was conducting his regular telephone interview program one night on WIOD, Miami, his guest was a representative from Women's Lib. A man called in, and the following conversation ensued:

MAN: Do you realize that all nature is set up in pecking orders?

WOMAN: Yes, and I know that in many animals, the female is at the top of the pecking order.

MAN: But it's a minority.

MERRILL: (interrupting) All right, then what you're saying is that, according to you, in all nature, the man is the pecker and the woman is the peckee.

Cutie Pie

The following was heard on KUTY, Palmdale, California. "On the local news scene the shitty sherriff, I mean the city sheriff, was kept busy with three buglers last night . . . burglars!"

Even Steven

On a particularly lively edition of the NBC-TV Today Show, Edmund Muskie repeatedly referred to host Bill Monroe as "Frank McGee." Listeners were doubly confused when Mr. Monroe began calling Muskie "Senator McGovern."

An Ill Wind

This poor weathercaster made the following remarks about hurricane Agnes: "And as you already know, Agnes really blew the whole city this afternoon."

Peter Piper Picked a Peck of . . .

I wonder what kind of response the local law enforcement people got when a radio station public service announcer read that the police department was in need of "parking peter maids."

Change of Announcer

Overheard on a local television station break: "We'll be right back, after this menopause . . . minute pause!!"

A Beaut

Sometimes a single incorrect letter in a news story can change the entire meaning of a sentence. A copywriter in the midwest was out of a job after giving the newscaster an item which read as follows:

ANNOUNCER: . . . meanwhile, in Rome, a large number of Catholics are petitioning to have the late Pope beautified . . . uh, I believe that should be "beatified."

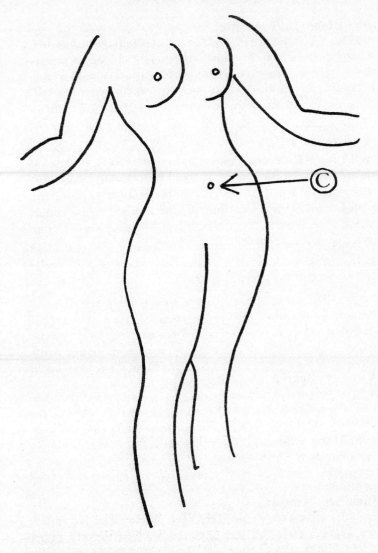

Novel Idea
LOUELLA PARSONS: It is rumored here in Hollywood that
the film company bought the rights to a new navel for Audrey
Hepburn.

No Place Like Home

Heard on "The Edge Of Night": An actor, having just been discharged from the hospital, where he had spent several months lying on his back with a serious illness, looks around the family surroundings and happily exclaims to his wife, "Mary, oh it's so good to be homo . . . (gulp) . . . home."

A Pair of Cities

A well-known Hollywood movie gossip commenator came out with this gem of a Blooper: ". . . and from Rome comes word of a new movie scheduled to go into production soon, starring Sophia Loren. Several locations for the film are being considered for Miss Loren . . . among them Florence and Nipples, Italy . . . er . . . Naples."

Ace in the Hole

"And we disc jockeys have made a special plaque which will go to any golfer who notifies us when he has scoled a hore in one!"

Charity Begins at Home

The following was heard on "The Joey Bishop Show." Joey was telling a socialite guest that he remembered that she was the sponsor of a charity event. Joe innocently asked, "By the way, how was your affair . . . er . . . I mean, tell us about your latest affair."

Jack Be Nimble

Jack Paar appeared in an NBC-TV special entitled "Jack Paar's Diary." Jack had just surfaced from a car submerged in about fifteen feet of water. He was taking a lesson on surviving if his car fell in. He surfaced and started telling about it. Scheduled next was a cut to a commercial, but apparently they stayed on him too long. A few seconds before the commercial, Paar said, "Let's get the hell out of here!"

Communication Gap

Mayor Daley of Chicago was being interviewed on television following the riots during the Democratic convention. The mayor stated "The police in Chicago are not here to create disorder, they are here to preserve it."

Something to Celebrate

During the course of a television documentary, the following was heard: "The Lord Mayor's Show, which celebrates the erection of the new Lord Mayor of London, takes place annually in November . . . that should read *election.*"

Ho, Ho, Ho

Station Promotion: "Tonight, it's Bing Crosby and Carol Burnett. See the Christmas special starring Bing and Carol, together again for the first time . . . (OFF MIKE) . . . Hey, who wrote this promo?"

Try a Deodorant

Mike Douglas very often brings on a surprise guest unbeknownst to his co-host. In this instance, the co-host was popular singer-comedienne Pearl Bailey. The surprise guest turned out to be Louis "Satchmo" Armstrong, a very dear and old friend of Pearl's. Mike, probably influenced by Louis's traditional and constant mopping of his brow with his handkerchief, asked Armstrong, "What advice would you give young perspiring performers?"

The Long and Short of It

SPORTSCASTER: Here we are on the fifteenth green where Billy Casper is getting ready to putt . . . Billy, usually an excellent putter, seems to be having difficulty with his long putts. However, he has no trouble dropping his shorts.

Must Be a Convention

SPORTSCASTER: Today's professional football schedule has the Buffalo Bills at Denver, the Oakland Raiders at Denver and the Miami Dolphins at Denver . . . (OFF MIKE) . . . that sounds like a helluva lotta teams at Denver on one Sunday afternoon . . . where in the hell did we get this schedule?

Gigged

Dick Cavett wanted to tell about his guests for that night's show, when he came up with this Blooper: "Hi, I'm Dick Cavett, and tonight my guest is Academy Award Wimmer . . . Academy Award Wimmer . . . there . . . I've done it again . . . Academy Award Winer, Gig Young!"

Let's Be Buddies

President Nixon, on the campaign trail to win support for Republicans running for office in many states, arrived in Miami Beach, where he spoke to a huge throng on behalf of the candidate for the United States Senate, Bill Cramer. He raised the candidate's hand and told voters, "So be sure when election time rolls around next Tuesday, to vote for my old friend . . . er . . . Congressman Bull Craner!"

Screwy Commercial

Movie commercial: "So for a holiday treat you can take the entire family to see . . . this is one picture you will not want to miss. All of the nation's critics love Screws . . . I beg your pardon, that should be Scrooge."

Heads Up

DISC JOCKEY: And now, the hit song from Butch Cassidy and the Sundance Kid, starring Paul Newman, Bert Bacharach's beautiful ballad, "Rain Drops Keep Falling on My Bed!"

Paging Raquel Welch

Heard on the "Outdoor Life" Program: "Our first guest this afternoon is one of the nation's outstanding experts on birds, who has just returned from an extended trip to Australia. In addition to bringing back several parrots, she boasts of owning the largest parateets in captivity."

Nice Trick If You Can Do It
Heard on "The French Chef": "Then you add two forkfuls of cooking oil . . ."

Boy Wonder
During the course of an exciting Oakland Raiders-Kansas City Chiefs football game, sportscaster Curt Gowdy blooped, "The seventy-eight yard drive was led by fourteen-year-old veteran, Lenny Dawson!"

Surprise Party
NEWSCASTER: . . . and from Washington comes word that President and Mrs. Lincoln will spend Nixon's birthday at Key Biscayne, Florida, on February twelfth.

Flipp-Her
Popular TV and recording star, Glenn Campbell, was sitting on the edge of a small concrete fish pond, singing a duet with a female guest. At the end of the number, Glenn spread his arms out in a big finish. His singing companion went flying backwards, falling into the pond for an unexpected bath.

Game Called Because of Wetness
SPORTSCASTER: It's raining again, and it appears just a matter of minutes before play will be called because of the weather. As the Pittsburgh Pirates' pitcher stands on the mound, you can barely see the P.P. on his muddy uniform.

One Up
On the Tonight Show, Johnny Carson was telling how he disliked cabs and had walked to work that evening rather than take a taxi. He told viewers, "A cabbie drove by giving me a peace sign . . . half of which I returned."

A Knockout!

In March of 1969, heavyweight boxer Jerry Quarry won an important nationally-televised bout in Madison Square Garden. A station in Binghamton, New York, infuriated boxing fans by putting commercials between every round, in such a way as to cut off the last few seconds of one round and the first few seconds of the next. All the commercials were for a local sponsor . . . a Ford automobile agency. Imagine the whoops of delight when Quarry, interviewed by ringside commentator, Don Dunphy, stated that for winning the bout, he was receiving a new Pontiac from an Oakland, California dealer!

Hole in One

A disc jockey on KCBQ, San Diego was asking his listeners to call in and try to win a record album. He surprised the radio audience with the following: "All right, stick your finger in the operator's hole and . . . uh, the telephone hole marked operator, that is, and call in now."

Inflammatory Remark

On Channel 32, in Chicago, the evening announcer finished up a commercial for an arthritis relief ointment with this live closing . . . "For more inflammation read the label."

Car Sickness

NEWSCASTER: (READING HEADLINES) ". . . accident on freeway involves four cars, hospitalizes one . . ."

My Old Kentucky Home

WEATHERMAN: . . . and there is a high pressure system around Lexintuck, Kentuxy . . . I mean Lexington, Kentuxy . . . you know what I mean.

Chief Red in the Face
A BBC newsreader saved the day and probably his job when he caught himself just in time when reading the following news item about the Chief Constable of Kent: "It has been learned that the Chief Kenstable of . . . and now we turn to news in the world of sports."

Three's a Crowd
In a television interview several years ago, Senator Margaret Chase Smith of Maine was questioned about her presidential aspirations. Asked what she would do if she woke up one morning and found herself in the White House, she replied, "I would go straight downstairs and apologize to Mrs. Eisenhower, and then I would go right home."

Tinkle, Tinkle, Little Star
Pianist Roger Williams appeared on the Mike Douglas Show with Robert L. Green, fashion director for *Playboy* magazine. Green told Williams, "Although I have never met you, I've heard you tinkling many times." Williams came back with, "I've been tinkling since I was a little child."

Oh Mummy!
NEWSCASTER: Enthusiasts from far and wide journeyed hundreds of miles to queue up in some instances for more than six hours outside the British Museum to get a look at King Tutankhamun, the famous mammy.

Do You Still Beat Your Wife?
On the Perry Mason program, Walter Pidgeon, substituting for Raymond Burr, addressed the witness in the following manner: "Answer this question with a simple yes or no . . . what were your feelings toward the murdered man?"

Cool, Man, Cool

Commercial: "This king-size refrigerator is large enough to seat all the nudes of your family . . . suit all the needs of your family!!!"

TV Daddy
Mike Douglas often becomes victim to spoonerisms, unintended interchanges of syllables. One such lapse occurred when he had Milton Berle as his guest. Mike was seriously relating many of Milton's valuable contributions to television, when he said, "Milton, we owe you a gret of dadditude."

'Nuff Said
Heard on ABC-TV's Newlywed Game: "What one thing have you mastered since you have been married?" "Sex."

Aloha
Sportscaster Chris Schenkel was broadcasting the football game between the college all-stars in the annual Hula Bowl game, which was played in Hawaii and beamed to fans nationwide by satellite. Also part of the broadcast team was former Oklahoma football coach Bud Wilkerson and All-American football great O. J. Simpson. A TV camera switched to a pretty coed in the stands, which prompted Schenkel to ask, "Bud, isn't that the young lady who gave us a lei before the game?"

Help!
Barbara Walters, one of the co-emcees on the NBC "Today" show, had talented actress Mercedes McCambridge as her guest. Miss McCambridge was to tell of her gallant victory over alcohol. The well-meaning and usually reliable Barbara told her viewers that her guest was at one time "in dire need of trouble."

Hands Off
Heard on a Smothers Brothers summer show. Just before a commercial break, the announcer blurted out, "Don't play with your knob . . . we'll be right back!"

I'm Not Thirsty

TV personality David Frost was discussing the problems of pollution on his syndicated TV program. He told how important he thought it was for pollution inspectors to "personally pass drinking water."

Out of This World

Heard on "Star Trek," popular science fiction series, when Captain Kirk, the hero, fell in love with a woman who was plotting to destroy a planet: "Millions of people who have never died before will be killed."

Ball Carriers

SPORTSCASTER: The half-back takes a pitchout and is immediately hit behind the line of scrimmage by a crunching, vicious tackle . . . it's a fumble and there are a couple of loose balls on the field.

Slips Don't Count

The emcee on "The Newlywed Game" asked the husbands what size bed they had in the bridal suite on their honeymoon. One of the new grooms confidently blurted out, "A double bed . . . and I know I'm right because we were so used to a king-size bed" . . . which made the bride hide her face during the rest of the program.

Can't Tell Players Without a Scorecard

NEWSCASTER: Also present at the rally were Governor and Mrs. Governor Ronald Reagan . . . that is, Mrs. Governor and Mr. Reagan . . . (exasperated) . . . California's first lady and his wife . . . oh, well . . . I'm sure you know who I mean!

Ball Breaker
A BBC radio announcer apparently had too much holiday spirit, with the following result . . . "We now hear Deck Your Balls With Halls of Helly . . . Deck Your Bells With Balls of Holly . . . er . . . a Christmas selection."

A Lot of Bull
NEWSCASTER: It is the opinion of many observers, that in handling the situation, the President hit the bull's eye on the nose.

When You Gotta Go——
Arlene Francis, popular femcee and panelist on What's My Line, was doing a studio audience warm-up on radio many years ago. She miscalculated the allotted time and said: "There are thirty seconds to go, if anyone has to." This advice was heard by millions of her listeners."

Nuts to You
In his anxiety to please his new sponsor, Chock Full of Nuts, on NBC-TV, popular comedian, Morey Amsterdam, tripped over the client's name and spurted out, "You will enjoy a Jock Full of Nuts Special at lunchtime."

Gentle on My Mind
Station promo: "This Sunday, see the adventures of an Everglades family and a bear, on Gentile Ben . . . that, of course, should be Gentle Ben."

Half Time
Station break: "We will return to the third half of the Virginian in a moment."

I'm up and see me sometime!

Wild, Wild West

On the "Merv Griffin Show," Arch Obler was talking about the time he had written an Adam and Eve sketch which was to star Mae West. Obler was talking about Miss West's unusual method of making transactions, writing checks and doing business, when he blooped: "I said that because Mae West does all her business in her bedroom. I mean she does everything in her bedroom . . . Now I'm getting in deeper!"

For the Birds
ANNOUNCER: At 8 P.M. we will present another in the series of classic dramatizations as part of this month's Shakespearian festival. Tonight's presentation is Macbeth, considered by many to be the greatest work of the Bird of Avon.

Sex and the Single Girl
NEWSCASTER: The C-47, carrying a planeload of chorus girls bound for a USO destination to entertain troops, was forced down in a jungle somewhere in Africa . . . However, all parsons abroad were reported safe."

I've Got a Secret
Art Linkletter has learned that children don't have many secrets. Just to make conversation, he recently asked a little girl what her mother had told her not to do that day. "She told me not to announce that she was pregnant."

Just Ducky
NEWSCASTER: . . . and Florida's candidate for governor, Reuben Askew, accused incumbent Governor Claude Cluck . . . er Kirk of ducking the issue.

Hello, Canada!
Larry Mann was doing an interview program from Toronto. One night his guests were Jane Mansfield and Mickey Hargitay, her husband. Mann was questioning Jayne about her early career and her financial problems. He leaned forward, starring straight at Jayne, who was, as usual, wearing an extremely low-cut dress, and said, "Tell me, though, Jayne, has there ever been a time when you were flat busted?" Jayne just sat there and couldn't say a word.

Jokers Wild

People in broadcasting have to have a sense of humor to survive April Fool's Day, which brings a rash of pranks to unsuspecting victims. Here is one such case where an unsuspecting weather forecaster was handed the following weather information: "Here's tomorrow's weather forecast: heavy snowfall predicted in the Valley Forge area, which is expected to retard General Washington's troops . . . (OFF MIKE) . . . all right, who's the wise guy?"

Mama Mia!

DISC JOCKEY: . . . and for all of you Cass Elliot fans, here are her big ones on a brand new platter . . . uh . . . here are her big ones . . . er . . . from her brand new album titled 'Mama's Big Ones' . . . (OFF MIKE) . . . whew, that's a mouthful!

By Cracky

The radio station manager, who doubled as salesman and announcer, was reading a commercial for a local grocery store for the upcoming weekend. The fluff he committed went like this: "Remember, ladies, Modern Cash Grocery is featuring special prices for your weekend meal planning . . . And don't forget to stop up on graham crappers."

Truth and Consequences

Ralph Edwards was telling Mike Douglas about the time veteran newsman Lowell Thomas was the surprise guest on "This Is Your Life." The all-too-honest Thomas described the proceedings as a "sinister conspiracy." To make matters worse, the confused Edwards said, "Lowell, I know you are going to enjoy tonight's surprise." To which Lowell snapped back with an annoyed look, "I doubt it!"

No Sex, Please, We're British

ANNOUNCER: "Tonight on BBC, Keith Michell, starring in television's award-winning presentation of King Henry VIII, a dramatization of the life and loves of this provocative monarch and his sex wives . . . *six* wives!"

A Real Pip

A disc jockey on a university campus radio station introduced a recording by Gladys Knight and the Pips with the following: "And now, rock 'n' roll fans, here's a new record by Gladys Knight and the Pimps!"

Just the Facts, Please

On a Dragnet program about an extortionist, Sergeant Friday interviewed a man who had been swindled out of a large sum of money. The man was hesitant to prosecute, because he feared for his family's safety. He nervously told Friday, "You don't understand, I have a wife and three kids, all under twelve ."

Daze of the Month

Usually reliable Walter Cronkite drew a complete blank at the close of one of his nightly news programs. He turned to the TV camera, as he had done countless times in the past and said, "And that's the way it is . . . on this . . . what day is this? . . . Oh, yes . . . October sixteenth . . . (laughing) . . . Good-night!"

Hard Headed

Quiz program: "Our next contestant is a Mr. Harwell of Knightsbridge. He works in the meat department of a Safeway Market, where he is the hard butcher . . . I mean he is the *head* butcher!"

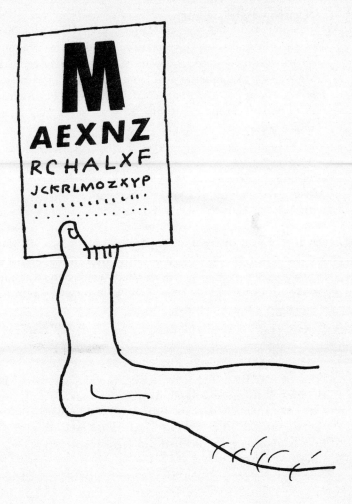

Cockeyed

The host of a local talk show in the mid-west confused his viewers when he told them: "Our next guest is a prominent optometrist, Dr. Harold Levy, who will be talking to us about diseases of the feet."

Learn, Baby, Learn

Consumer crusader Ralph Nader appeared on "The Mike Douglas Show." The conversation centered on Nader's findings concerning alleged false nutrition claims. He said, "For instance, we are looking into some of the claims made by a leading booby foob company." Mike snapped back with, "You had better be careful what you say . . . there may be a lot of boobies watching this show."

Shady Lady

Musical comedy star Carol Channing appeared as a guest with Johnny Carson on his Tonight Show. When it came for him to do a latex paint commercial, he held up the sponsor's product. Carol interrupted to tell how she had used the paint and found it to be very good. Johnny replied, "You see, an ordinary lady we picked up off the street." After the audience roared, Johnny apologized, "Come, now, you know I don't mean that kind of lady."

Blackout

NEWSCASTER: The coal strike is growing worse here in Britain, with more and more workers walking out, and it is expected that the pickets will cause a complete shitdown of the mines . . . that should read *shutdown*. It also appears that sympathetic unions will not cross picnic lines . . . picket lines!

Illegitimate Announcement

Remotes, the programs originating away from the station, give rise to embarrassing and ridiculous situations, such as the time an announcer confidently announced the name of the last selection as "performed by Lex Bastard and his orchestra . . . Lex Baxter!"

A Broad Statement
Christine Jorgenson appeared as a guest on The Mike Douglas Show, after an extensive trip. Mike innocently asked Miss Jorgenson how long she was "abroad," much to the delight of a chuckling audience.

To Your Health
The announcer was doing a commercial for a local drug store, plugging their sale on Vigram vitamins: "So, mothers, give all the members of your family Vigram vitamins to keep them fit and filthy . . . uh . . . healthy!"

Goosy
"The American League standings show the Cleveland Indians in first place with the New York Yankees close up there behind."

Falling Flat on His Ear
Ad libs do not always come off as cleverly as intended. One day, TV's "Galloping Gourmet" decided to "play my next recipe by ear . . . when you are married, it's about the only thing left to play with."

Station Break
Steve Allen was demonstrating the virtues of a non-breakable fibreglass chair on the Tonight Show. The manufacturer had told him to take a hammer and strike the chair as hard as he wished. After the first whack, pandemonium broke loose when he poked a hole right through the chair . . . He bailed himself out by ad libbing: "Well, anyway, this hammer is made of fibreglass."

Open Heart Surgery

D.J. Chris Musk, on Manx Radio, operating in the British Isles, tells the following: A pop version of the well-known hymn "All Things Bright and Beautiful" was going out over the air (artist, Joe Brown). As the record faded, the announcer stated that whenever he went to church services he always looked forward to singing along to the more stirring hymns because one could then "open up your *bowels* and sing forth." The chief announcer immediately phoned in to say: "You open up your heart, not your bloody arse!"

Sour Grapes

Commercial: "So remember, if you have that tired, letdown feeling after a long hot day . . . Welchade Grape is a hell of a way to refresh yourself . . . (PAUSE) . . . you know, of course, this fine drink is a *healthy* way to refresh yourself."

In a Pickle

QUIZMASTER: All right, you have now won fifty silver dollars. Now for one hundred silver dollars, you are to finish the following . . . Are you ready now? Peter Piper-----
CONTESTANT: Pickled Peckers!

Big Man

On What's My Line, Arlene Francis asked the mystery guest if he was a male. Blindfolded guest panelist, Vincent Price, after hearing the guest's voice, chimed in, "All male from stem to stern!"

Have You Got a Wrong Number?

EMCEE: Well, that just about wraps up another Telephone Quiz program for tonight. Tune in again tomorrow at the same time when I'll be crawling on you again!

Sounds Like Dean Martin
During the televised Watergate hearings, former White House legal advisor, John Dean, was questioned about the exact nature of some of his official duties. His surprising answer was: "You might say I was there to make sure all the i's were crossed and the t's were dotted."

Food for Thought
NEWS ANNOUNCER: Consumer advocate Ralph Nader is in the news again. Nader, who first achieved prominence when he attacked the manufacturers of booby foods . . . baby foobs . . . foods, is now going after General Motors. According to Nader, GM had advance tits . . . tips about Nixon's price freeze.

What's in a Name?
A contestant on an audience participation program had the misfortune of being from a suburb of Falmouth, Massachusetts, called Woods Hole. When the host of the show accidently pronounced Falmouth as "foulmouth," the nervous guest tried to correct him: "No, it's *Falmouth,* but actually I'm from Ass Hole, Woodsachusetts."

Paging Mr. Ripley!
NEWSMAN: And now we switch you to Police Headquarters downtown for further developments on the Mary Harkness Case.

POLICEMAN: This is Police Sergeant Edward O'Reilly. The parents of Mary Harkness have asked the police to search for their daughter, who has been missing since 6 P.M. yesterday. She was last seen wearing a blue sweater and gray skirt. Mary is 99 years old and weighs 9 pounds.

From the Chandelier
Veteran Kansas broadcaster Charley Whitworth reports that, on one particularly hectic night at one of the Wichita TV stations, a novice announcer spieled this gem for the Overhead Door Company: "This special on home-type garage doors ends Saturday at five P.M. at the Overdead Whore Company."

Mr. Lucky

Movie actress Honor Blackman was on a promotional tour, plugging the film "Goldfinger" in which she had the role of Pussy Galore. She visited radio and TV stations, where she was interviewed. When she was interviewed on KGO-TV, her enthusiastic interviewer remarked, "I've covered topless bathing suits, bottomless bathing suits, and now I've got Pussy Galore!"

Bad News

NEWSCASTER: Good evening. It's time for the six P.M. news. Tonight's big story is the devastating flood in East Pakistan, brought to you by your Chevrolet dealers.

Could Be

SPORTSCASTER: Before the upcoming New York Jets-Baltimore Colts football championship, scheduled to be played next week at the Super Bowl, Coach Ewbank called his star quarterback, Joe Namath, the most offensive player in football . . . best offensive player.

That'sa Nice

"So for a heavenly Italian dinner, that your entire family will enjoy, try Chef Boy-ar-dee Marijuana Sauce . . . marinara sauce!"

Fore!

The Philadelphia Eagles have a star quarterback whose name is Norm Snead. However, the play-by-play football announcer, an ardent golfer, got his sports mixed up when he observed "Going back to pass to his tight end is Sam Snead."

Splitting Headache

JACK PAAR: (FINISHING COMMERCIAL) . . . so remember, try Bufferin. Boy, do I have a terrible headache . . . I bet I took nine aspirin . . . *Bufferin!!!*

Double Talk

Heard on David Susskind's TV discussion program, "Open End": "I may not always be right, but I'm never wrong."

A Bachelor

ART LINKLETTER: You look like a cute little boy. I would judge you to be around three or four years old. Do you have any brothers or sisters?
BOY: No, I am single.

It's a Treat to Beat Your Meat

A hostess for a daily housewives' hints TV program was talking about the storing of meat in the freezer. After demonstrating how to prepare the meat for freezing, she went into methods for using frozen meat. Her lead-in was: "Now ladies, you take your meat out of the freezer and beat it!"

He's a Scream

SPORTSCASTER: And Joe Namath screams to his tight end . . . uh, that should be *screens,* folks!

Spitz It Out

We wonder what was going on in the mind of the radio announcer who gave his listeners this memorable line: "Stay tuned for an exclusive interview with Olympipic swimming star, Mark Spritz."

Piggy Back
Commercial: "This new Dodge pickup will hold a real pig family . . . that should be *big* family!"

Good Advice
ANNOUNCER: The Mike Douglas Show from Cypress Gardens, Florida, is arranged by the Florida Citrus Commission, who recommends that you start your day off right getting juiced . . . I mean start your day with a glass of Orange Juice.

The Cat's Meow
Johnny Carson had as his guest a woman who ran a cattery—an establishment for the care and sale of cats. Johnny shook up his late night viewers with, ". . . and in a little while we are going to bring out a lady who runs a cat house."

Keeping Up with the Joneses
Ed Sullivan, talking briefly to Jack Jones after his spot on the Sunday night TV program, asked, "Wasn't Alan Jones your father?" "He still is," snapped the Jones boy.

There's Many a Slip Twixt the Cup and the Lip
A London announcer, giving the day's program schedule, blooped the following . . . "At 1:45, London Weekend brings viewers 'University Challenger,' followed at 2:15 by an in-depth leak into the F.A. Cup . . . *look* into the F.A. Cup final . . . I beg your pardon!"

Lousy Weather
WEATHER FORECASTER: The weather forecast for New Orleans and vicinity is partly clousy and tatered shunder towers.

Shut Out

Allen Ludden described one of the contestents on his program, Password, in the following manner: "We now have a female contestant with 33 years of happy marriage, and no score yet . . . uh, in the game."

Odd Couple

While introducing her guest, Jack Klugman, Carol Burnett mentioned that at one time "Jack was Ethel Merman's leading lady . . . ah, leading man!"

Curt Remark

During the 1971 World Series, sports enthusiasts across the country tried to figure out what Curt Gowdy meant when he said, "Brooks Robinson is not a fast man, but his arms and legs move very quickly."

Inside Story

In an interview with astronaut John Glenn, a newsman asked what the toughest part of his training was. Glenn thought a moment, then answered: "That's a tough one, and it's hard to choose one in particular, but if you think of how many openings there are on the human body, and . . . uh, how far you can go in any one of them, you tell me which was the hardest test."

Playboy

A KPHO-TV announcer in Phoenix, Arizona, startled listeners when his voice came over a preview of a Star Trek episode. The preview showed several scantily-clad curvaceous, bunny-type females dancing in a harem-type surrounding, and the local announcer came in with, "Opie joins a secret club on the Andy Griffith Show, next on KPHO-TV."

Sneaky Pete
Listeners must have wondered what the KLOC, California, announcer, Peter Boyle, meant when he gave the weather and marine forecast, and advised about "small crafty warnings."

Hear, Hear!
During the Freedom 7 space shot, two technicians from Houston were overheard by millions of listeners:

FIRST TECHNICIAN: How is it, Charley?
SECOND TECHNICIAN: I don't know . . . I can't hear a thing on this goddamn phone!

Blankety Blank
Station promo: "Monday is inauguration day . . . stay tuned to this channel and see Nixon *swearing* on the steps of the Capitol in Washington."

Getting to the Bottom of Things
When Jackie Joseph was a guest on the Virginia Graham Show, she wore a particularly short dress. When the hostess asked her about it, Miss Joseph replied, "People kept asking me what I was going to wear, and it's the first time I've ever exposed my bottom half . . . I mean my *legs* on television!"

Urgent Needs
When Peter Lawford was doing his "Dear Phoebe" impression of love-lorn columnists on the Mike Douglas Show, he asked for questions from the audience. A fifteen-year-old boy stood up and started to relate the problems he was having with his wife. Douglas cut in and said, "You're only fifteen? You must have married at an early urge . . . age!"

Hair Today, Gone Tomorrow
Commercial: "So remember, Hidden Magic Shampoo puts hair on your body . . . that should be 'Remember, Hidden Magic Shampoo puts body in your hair!'"

X Rated

On a Hollywood Squares program, Joey Bishop was asked to name the various performers who had played in different versions of "Dr. Jekyll and Mr. Hyde" throughout the years. After telling the names of the stars in the first two versions of the film, Bishop concluded with: ". . . and in 1932, Spencer Tracy did it with Ingrid Bergman."

The Old College Try

A sports announcer in Buffalo, New York goofed: ". . . and the penalty against Yale brings it back to the Yarvard twenty hard line."

Virgin Territory

An anouncer at WRR-FM, Dallas, Texas, blooped the following: "Tonight see Eugene O'Neill's 'Long Day's Journey Into Night,' brought to you in its original, uncut virgin."

Red, White and Lavender

Steve Allen, substituting for Dick Cavett, decided to take one of the studio cameras out on the street to photograph people. The camera swung around to an old fire station with a flag hanging listlessly in the still air. Allen commented: "And you can tell there's very little wind in New York today by looking at that limp fag . . . uh, flag."

No Bones About It

WRC-TV, Maryland, carried a live commercial in which the announcer blooped: "This week's meat special is delicious bottomless bottom round roast . . . make that *boneless* bottom round roast."

Having a Ball

Performers in broadcasting can sometimes be the victims of unintended double meanings. Such was the case on a popular children's program on BBC radio, entitled Music and Movements for Infants, presided over by the talented and capable Margery Eel. This innocent double entendre perked up listeners' ears and has since become a classic in the world of broadcasting . . . "Today we are going to play a hiding and finding game with music . . . We are going to pretend that you have got some balls and I am going to hide them . . . The music will tell you where your balls are . . . They may be high up on the ceiling . . . or low down on the floor . . . Now stand up and dance around looking everywhere for your balls . . . I hope that you have found your balls . . . Now toss them in the air and play with them."

He Can't See the Forest

A spoonerism is defined by Webster as an unintended interchange of syllables. It was just that type of blooper that cost an announcer his job when he read a promo about a movie starring Forest Tucker.

Double Trouble

Heard on KLIF radio, Dallas: "There has been a rash of armed robberies in the city, five within the past two hours . . . Two short-armed rubbers . . . robbers held up a bank this morning."

Which End Is Up?

The following blooper was broadcast from Cape Kennedy: "This is mission control at NASA. Apollo Fourteen seems to be experiencing difficulty with a low-voltage battery located at the ass end of the lunar module . . . aft-end!"

Relax and Enjoy It

A channel 5, Atlanta, novice announcer shocked his viewing audience with a report that, "a state prisoner has been transferred to the central mental hospital because he is considered to be an encourageable rapist."

A Fish Story

A North Carolina restaurant, The City Shellfish, will never be the same, since an announcer inadvertently read their commercial thusly: "So, come to the Shitty Selfish, I mean Silly Shitfish . . . oh, hell . . . back to the news!"

Slips That Pass in the Night

While doing a commercial for a leading fabric softener, Ed McMahon was supposed to have slid a pin through a diaper, while saying, "See how easy it is to pass through." Unfortunately, when air time came, he stabbed the pin into the diaper and told startled viewers, "See how easy it is to pee through."

Clean It Up

Heard on a TV special about pollution: "For each ounce of water they find seven hundred and fifty orgasms . . . heavens, that should be organisms!"

Guest Who's Coming to Dinner?

The hostess of a local women's program was listing a number of easy casseroles for the working mother to prepare, when she began extolling the virtues of these one-dish meals:

"And one of the nice things about these casseroles is that they have wide appeal to many sordid guests . . . that is, *assorted* guests."

8-COUNT EM-8

Age Before Beauty
On a popular audience participation program, a pretty young
lady contestant was asked for the definition of an octogenarian.
She immediately snapped back with . . . "Oh, I know . . .
an octogenarian is a person with eight toes."

Fumble

Johnny Carson introduced a commercial on the Tonight Show thusly: "And now, friends, we're going to show you how vinyl paneling is tougher than Ray Nitschke of the Green Bay Pickers!"

Come Again?

The armed forces radio network in Vietnam broadcast a story about scientific findings on the Apollo flight to the moon. The announcer read the story as follows: ". . . and the scientists' reports show that the moon rocks may contain living orgasms . . . uh, excuse me, that's supposed to be that the moon rocks have living *organisms*."

White on White

Cousin Duffy, giving weather information on his WMEX Ski Report, said: "And there's a chance of snow mixed with snow later on tonight."

Shop Fast!

Silver Springs, Maryland listeners must have been a little surprised when a local announcer told them to "take advantage of Levitz's sixty-second anniversary sale . . . that is, they've been in business for sixty-two years."

London Bridge Is Falling Down

NEWSCASTER: Queen Victoria was today seen pissing over Westminster Bridge on her way to Buckingham Palace.

Please Be Patient

With the increasing popularity of medical discussion programs, doctors are finding it isn't enough just to be a com-
petent surgeon. Many of them are having to brush up on
public speaking, to avoid Bloopers like the following:

HOST: So how many patients do you think would be the
maximum for one nurse?
DR.: Generally speaking, there shouldn't be more than seven
patients in a hospital bed for each nurse on duty.

With Lox

Station promo: "See the New York Jets play the Cincinnati Bagels this Sunday on NBC . . . I mean Bengals!!"

Good Show

An announcer on the BBC in England told his audience that he had an exclusive interview in store for them. He stated that he was going to present films at 9 P.M. that evening showing him "queering the Queen just before the Coronation . . . I beg your pardon . . . I meant querying the Queen!"

Child Bride

Art Linkletter was interviewing a group of six- and seven-year-olds on "People Are Funny." Coming to one little girl, he asked, "And what age would you like to be?" "Twelve," answered the girl. "Oh, that's an interesting age to be," he replied. "And why do you want to be twelve?" "Because my Mommy's twelve!" replied the little girl. "My," snickered Art, "we sure have some strange marriages nowadays!"

Cross Your Heart

Heard on the morning "Dick Van Dyke Show": "This program has been brought to you by Playtex Loving Bra . . . Living Bra!"

Nuff Said

Playing Stump the Band on the "Tonight" Show, Johnny Carson called on a woman in the audience for her musical selection. When she stood up, she appeared quite large in the midsection.

CARSON: You are?
WOMAN: Yes!

at the Beach –

Get the Picture?
Commercial: "You can get this attractively priced camera at Mel's . . . it's guaranteed to take pictures in either black or white."

Flucked Again
NEWSCASTER: According to Enoch Powell, Member of Parliament from Wolverhampton, the pound will suffer further fucktuation before it stabilizes!

She Hasn't the Foggiest
A BBC woman announcer doing a weather forecast read the copy from the telex, which accidently eliminated the letter "f" in fog. Caught by surprise, she told her audience . . . "I am sorry to have to inform you that there is no f . . . in fog."

Cold Shoulder
An interesting commentary was perpetuated by Britain's own Henry Cooper when he was talking about the controversial Sonny Liston retirement in the world championship fight against Cassius Clay, or Muhammed Ali. Henry remarked that Liston had a "very unusual injury . . . a dislocated soldier!"

Quite a Switch
EMCEE: Our next contestant has a job with a fine newspaper. She is a switchblade operator with the Toledo Broad . . . I mean switchboard operator with the Toledo Blade . . . I beg your pardon, young lady.

Night-mare
Allen Ludden, emcee of the popular television program, "Password," was telling his TV audience about the show's move to another night in the week, when he came out with this classic: "Just remember, folks, next Monday night 'Password' will be seen on Thursday evening!"

Birds Do It

Merv Griffin, on Play Your Hunch, told a visiting guest star, "We sure thank you for taking time out from your busy sexual . . . I mean schedule."

We Heard You the First Time

Election returns: "It is a very close race here in the eleventh district, and it's beginning to look as though Mayor Bailey, the incompetent, will be defeated! . . . (PAUSE) . . . I apologize to his honor, the mayor, the *incumbent*."

Tom, Dick or Harry

Elizabeth Taylor and Richard Burton appeared in an exclusive interview on the David Frost Show. In a serious moment, David queried, "Now that you have all of the material things of life, what do you want most, a baby by Richard?" Liz came back with, "Who else?"

A Good Sport

This sports commentator should have left well enough alone instead of trying to correct himself:

"Good evening, sports fans; we're crammed into a field house where tonight's sexual competition begins, with the State High School championship . . . did I say sectional? . . . I meant sexual."

Smashing!

SPORTSCASTER: And now stand by for a running of the exciting annual race car event, the Grand Pricks. . . er Grand Pee . . . however the hell you pronounce it . . . I'll give you the spelling and you take your choice. Grand P-R-I-X!

Sore Spot

When Hollywood's version of F. Scott Fitzgerald's "Tender Is The Night" finally came to television, one local announcer renamed it.

ANNOUNCER: Tune in at seven tonight for the Channel 5 movie. See Jason Robards in "Tendonitus."

Red Faced

During coverage of a Harvard basketball game, the local sports announcer blurted out the following: "And Harvard keeps on rolling up the score! It looks like nothing can stop the crappy scrimson team . . . er, *scrappy crimson* team!"

The Rain in Spain

DISC JOCKEY: And now we hear the ever-popular "Singing in the Wayne" sung by former Hit Parader, Bea Rain.

Out to Pastor

On his first Sunday "Service of the Air," the young pastor was extremely nervous. The sermon was going well until he came to the tenth commandment and advised both parishoners and radio listeners,"Thou shalt not cover thy neighbor's wife, nor his maidservant, nor his ox, nor his ass."

Air Time

Back in the 1930's, Decca Records had a 78 rpm record release by "Whoopee John and his Orchestra." The record label carried the full name of Whoopee John Wilfahrt, which caused one poor announcer to bloop: "And now, Whoopee John Wilfahrt and the Orchestra will play."

Making an Ass of Himself

This Blooper was contributed by Peter Marshall, host of the Hollywood Squares game show. He was paraphrasing one of Emily Post's rules of etiquette when he said: "When a man is finished smoking a cigar, should he leave his butt in the asstray? . . . I mean leave his butt in the *ash*tray!"

T'ain't Funny, McGee

On the NBC-TV Today Show, Frank McGee was speaking about the Supreme Court decision against capital punishment: "Currently on death row in this country are Sirhan Sirhan, assassin of Robert Kennedy, Richard Speck, who was found guilty of the murder of seven nurses, and Charles Manson of the Sharon Turd maters . . . Sharon Tate murders."

Moving Story

Tiny Tim was a guest on the Mike Douglas Show, when he told the audience he had lost forty pounds on a diet of onions and prune juice. Host Douglas commented, "Well, that ought to keep you moving." The audience broke up, and Douglas tried to cover the Blooper by saying, "I mean from place to place."

And That's the Way It Is

Even experienced newscasters like Walter Cronkite can make mistakes, as evidenced by the remarks he made after the late President Eisenhower returned from a vacation in Florida: "Apparently the Florida vacation did him a lot of good. Ike returned today looking fanned and tit . . that is, tanned and fit."

One Liner

ANNOUNCER: And now, here's the laugh king of the one-winer, Henny Youngman.

Thrown for a Loss

NBC sportscaster Charles Jones reported to surprised football enthusiasts that Joe Namath was "20 yards underweight."

An Orgy
All action disintegrated into hysterical laughter on the Tonight Show one evening, when beautiful, blonde Carol Wayne
told Johnny, "I had my first big affair; I had forty people."

A Run for Your Money
ANNOUNCER: Stay tuned for our Late Show movie stars
Laurence Harvey and Lee Remick in *The Running Man,*
brought to you tonight by Ex-Lax.

Floored!
During NBC's coverage of the 1972 Republican Convention,
John Chancellor made reference to NBC's "floorless fear reporters." He attempted to correct himself, but this time it
came out "fearless four reporters." Finally he admitted, "I
can't say it. I couldn't at the Democratic Convention, either."

Policemen's Ball
Pity the poor newsman who found himself out of a job, after
reading this story on the air: "In a concentrated effort to ap-
prehend the rapist, local police have asked all women in the
area to copulate with them . . . uh, that is to *cooperate* with
them."

Hold That Tiger!
WXYZ-TV Sportscaster, Dave Diles, learned about the pitfalls
of live interviews the hard way. After a Detroit Tigers winning game, he went back into the locker room to talk to the
celebrating players. He asked Tiger Eddie Brinkman how he
felt about the successful game, and was told, "It's a fantastic
feeling, not so much for myself, but for the rest of the f---in'
guys."

Leave the Driving to Us
NEWSCASTER: Plans were announced for the parade which will follow the Governor's conference. At 2 P.M. the cars will leave their headquarters just as soon as the Governors are loaded.

Doesn't Everybody?
On the popular Art Linkletter program, a youngster was asked what he wanted to be when he grew up. He replied, "A space man." He was then asked what he would do if he ran into a Martian. The youngster snapped back with, "I would say 'Excuse me.' "

Cape of Good Hope
At the opening of a new Hollywood movie in New York, a starlet who had just entered the lobby of the theater was described in this fashion by the commentator: "And now entering the lobby accompanied by her latest boyfriend is _____, and she is wearing a stunning muskrat rape!"

Private "I"
A fast-talking news announcer on WJAC-TV, Pennsylvania, read a story with follow-up information on the murder of union leader Joseph Yablonski:

ANNOUNCER: A .38 caliber revolver was found in the river today by FBA Igents.

One Hundred Percent Pure
Commercial: "So remember these remarkable statistics, and remember Crest, for the family that wants pure cavities!"

That's Rich
Governor Nelson Rockefeller of New York came out with this classic: "Take the typical unmarried woman of this State with three children . . ."

Paleface Speak With Forked-Up Tongue

After an exciting baseball game, the local sportscaster attempted to recap the action, with the following result: "Well, it took eleven Indians to beat the Cleveland innings, today!"

Girl Talk

NEWSCASTER: . . . and Lesbian Forces today attacked Israel . . . *Lebanese!*

The Cold Gray Mare Ain't What She Used to Be

WEATHER FORECASTER: And as we take a look at our weather map, we notice a cooler ass of mare sweeping in from Canada!

Late News

A California radio announcer blooped the following: "Stay tuned for the latest news, upcoming in six months . . . minutes!"

Get the Message

Jack Kelley, former host of NBC's Sale Of The Century, introduced a commercial as follows: "We're going to be back and resume our game in a very short message."

Time to Retire

Heard on the BBC: "As Big Ben's cock strikes eleven . . . it's time for the news!"

Vanishing Americans

NEWSCASTER: Here is a news bulletin from our newsroom. The federal government has ordered schools in Mississippi to disintegrate.

I Wonder Who's Kissinger Now

The news writer who put together the following story should have been a little more careful in his phrasing:

NEWSCASTER: On his way to the Vietnam Peace talks, Dr. Henry Kissinger made a stopover in Hawaii, where an attractive island girl gave him a lei.

A House Is Not a Home

The following lively exchange took place on an afternoon audience participation program:

HOST: And now, madame, before we let you select your category, is there anything you need to ask?

LADY: Yes, I'd like to ask you not to call me madame. Where I come from that refers to a woman who runs a house of ill-repute.

HOST: Oh really, madame?

Service With a Smile

Public service announcement overheard on a small New England radio station: "So if you need assistance with your call, just dial one-one-three, and a cheerful call girl will be at your service."

Racy

Joe Croghan, a Miami, Florida, sportscaster, once advised startled listeners to stay tuned for a video tape presentation of the running of the auto racing classic, the Grand Pee.

A New Twist

A lady pretzel baker making an appearance on the Tonight Show demonstrated to Johnny Carson and his late-night viewers the precise method of looping the dough to make the characteristic pretzel shape. Carson attempted to repeat her performance, but the dough didn't come out right. The lady gave him another strip of dough, saying, "Here, try this piece, I don't think yours was long enough. You can't do it if it's not the right length." The audience broke into hysterical laughter, and was just quieting down when Carson quipped, "Yes, I think I've heard that rumor before."

Welcome!

Freudian Slip
NEWSCASTER: On their way to a well-deserved vacation, Hubert Humphrey and Edmund Muskie stopped in Miami, en route to the Virgin Islands, and were visited by President-elect Nixon, who extended his hostility . . . I mean *hospitality* . . . to the defeated candidates.

Dog-Face Soldiers
PUBLIC SERVICE ANNOUNCER: "The local V.F.W. is sponsoring a dance at the civic center this Friday night at 8 p.m. Admission is one dollar per person, and all proceeds will go to the Veterinarians of Foreign Wars."

All Chucked Up
Chuck Conners was a guest on a women's afternoon TV program, when the hostess noticed there were only a few seconds left in which to close the show. She interrupted him with, "Well, I see our time is just about *up Chuck,* so we'll have to save it for the next time."

What's in a Name!
When Grampian Television was being formed in the British Isles, a proposed title was Scottish Highlands and Islands Television. This caused some consternation when one of the owners suggested that station S.H.I.T. would not be appropriate.

Easy? . . . No, Deeficult!
SPORTSCASTER: We have momentarily lost the video portion of our broadcast of the baseball game in which the Minnesota Twins are leading 2 to one . . . as soon as our difficulties are restored, we will resume the broadcast.

Coffee Break
The TV commercial announcer had given the news headlines, then in his juiciest and most churchlike tone he said: "More news in a minute, but first a word from Maxwell House Instant Coffee . . . Be sure to look for the jar with the stars on top . . . if you haven't tried it yet, I envy you!"

A Broad Statement
NEWSCASTER: You have just heard the news from in and around the nation . . . and now to Pauline Fredericks for the latest news from a broad!

Off the Cuff
When Karen and Richard Carpenter were the surprised guests on the "This Is Your Life" show, host Ralph Edwards gave them the traditional gifts given to guests on that program, a charm bracelet and a pair of cufflinks. Due to an unfortunate slip of the tongue, Edwards told the listening audience that the Carpenters would receive . . . "a gold charm bracelet for Karen, and brother Richard will get 'This Is Your Life' handcuffs."

Gay Deceivers?
NEWSCASTER: "United States Treasury Agents have announced their intentions to take a closer look into Swish Bank Accounts."

Sticky Fingers
WFIL radio in Philadelphia gave its listeners this surprising bit of public service information: "So hurry folks, and deposit your letters now. We'll be waiting for your droppings in the box."

Some Like It Hot
Blonde, buxom Carol Wayne wore a very revealing shorts and blouse ensemble on the Johnny Carson Tonight Show. When Johnny asked her if the outfit was considered to be "hot pants," Miss Wayne answered: "Yes, I've always had hot pants."

All Wet
NEWSCASTER: And fire commissioner Randolph Davis reported that his department fire-fighters poured over 2,000 gallons of gasoline on the blaze!

Knock Knock
ANNOUNCER: We have just received word from the courthouse that the jury is still out in the Lucy Brock paternity case, and it now looks like they will be knocked up for the night . . . that should be, locked up for the night!!!

Fares, Please
Commercial: "So get to your vacation spot fast and enjoy every fun-packed minute of it. Don't delay . . . call today and learn how to save money with Trans-American Airlines half-assed rates."

He Has One Tied On
SPORTSCASTER: And in the world of baseball: The Los Angeles Dodgers lead the San Francisco Giants 3-3 after eleven innings . . . I've got two words for this report . . . im-possible!!!

Maybe He Knows Something
ANNOUNCER: Good afternoon, ladies and gentlemen, and welcome to a program of songs sung by guest soprano Martha Bartow, who is a member of the Southern Methodist Glee Club here in Dallas. Miss Bartow is rated as one of the finest swingers here in the Southwest . . . of course, I mean *singers* in the Southwest!!

Trick or Treat

An Associated Press typographical error caused a mid-west announcer to read this unusual story to his listeners: "Many clergymen feel the recent avalanche of obscene material is a treat to young children . . . I'm sorry . . . that's a *threat* to young children!"

Jello, Everybody
Kid's show: "Now, kids, here is the delicious Soupy Sales Advertising Jello, which comes in many hilarious flavors."

Sterling Remark
On NBC's "You Don't Say," emcee Tom Kennedy said to Ann Jeffries, "I know who you were thinking of, Ann, you were probably thinking of your lovely wife, Bob Sterling . . . I mean, your lovely wife, Bob Jeffries."

Strained Remark
On the Merv Griffin Show, Virginia Graham asked Merv and Arthur Treacher if they carry grudges. Arthur Treacher replied that all he carried was a hernia!

A Nose for News
NEWSCASTER: We switch you to England for a report on the latest bombings in Belfast from Ray Sheerer, NBC's nose correspondent in London.

What a Man
SPORTSCASTER: . . . and leading the pike with a one-stroke lead, I mean pick . . . I mean *pack* . . . is Dick Sikes, who has a total of 281 after 54 hores . . . that should be holes!

Oh, Johnny
During one of Johnny Carson's monologues he stated: "You know on New Year's Eve most people are prone (AUDIENCE LAUGHS) . . . not that kind of prone . . . I mean susceptible to liquor!"

On Thin Ice
A confused hockey announcer on CBS's "Game of The Week" blurted out this startling bit of information: "I think he got the stick in the nose. He broke his nose earlier, and it looks as though it's the same nose that he injured before."

No Strings Attached
In an apparent effort to lull his listeners to sleep, Terry Smith of WOCN in Miami, Florida, told his audience to stay tuned for the sounds of "the Bobby Hackett Springs."

A Tight Squeeze
When Johnny Carson introduced his guest, composer Mac Davis, he credited the musician with having "a dozen songs in the top ten."

A Lot of Feeling
Dick Cavett had Dyan Cannon as his guest on his late night show. As she held his hand, he made this comment: "You're very touchy . . . uh, you're very touching . . . you touch a lot, don't you?"

Gave Proof Through the Nyet . . .
NBC's veteran newsman, John Chancellor, was covering President Nixon's trip to Moscow when he made this classic boner. As the President disembarked from the plane at Moscow Airport, a Russian band saluted him by playing the Star Spangled Banner.

CHANCELLOR: And as President Nixon steps down from the plane, a band has begun playing the Soviet National Anthem.

Whatcha Know, Joe

Movie star Joe E. Brown was pinch-hitting for Don McNeil on his ABC Breakfast Club. He interviewed a woman who told him she had four children. "That's your entire family, I suppose." "Hell no, there is a father too," she replied indignantly.

Indecent Exposure

A late night announcer got a call from a female listener who tried to guess what he looked like. After telling the radio audience that she thought the announcer was about six feet tall with sandy hair, she asked him how close she had come. He told her she was very close. Then the lady said, "I think I speak for all your listeners when I say we would like to see you exposed."

Severest Critic

On the TV kid show "TV Art and Crafts," the emcee asked a youngster the following: "Tell me, son, what do you think of your sister's painting?" The boy's answer was direct and to the point: "I think it's crappy!!!"

Bull Thrower

A contestant on "You Bet Your Life" was a bullfighter. He told emcee Groucho Marx that he had met more than three hundred bulls in the ring. Groucho snapped back with, "Young man, you must be the envy of every cow in Mexico!"

Poor Mother

NEWSCASTER: "Governor Nelson Rockefeller today vetoed a bill to repeal New York's 1970 liberalized abortion law, considered the most liberal in the nation. It permits a woman to have an abortion on request within the first twenty-four months of pregnancy."

Quack Quack
Heard on the BBC: "City fathers were hoping to raise enough money to erect a new bronze statue of the Duck of Wellington."

A Live One
ANNOUNCER: This prerecorded program has come to you live from Hollywood.

Bloody Good
Popular band leader Johnny Howard conducted a musical show titled "Easy Beat" on BBC radio for many years. The featured singer was Danny Street, now a popular recording artist. Danny was asked to introduced his next song which was written by Sam Coslow, titled "Everybody Loves Somebody Sometime." Danny blooped . . . "and now for a favorite song of mine and I am sure of yours . . . 'Everybloody Loves Somebloody Sometime.' "

Double Trouble
SPORTSCASTER: And the A's and the Rainsox were red out and will be played as part of next Sunday's double header on Thursday.

Women's Lib?
ANNOUNCER: We are proud to have with us today a woman who has been chosen as one of the most outstanding men in the United States.

X Marks the Spot
Sunny Ray of KIKK, Pasadena, Texas, was given a commercial at the last moment from the copy department. The spot was for a local outdoor theatre showing an X-rated film where absolutely no one under 18 would be admitted. This is what the listeners heard: "See all three of these big, adult-only features at the Red Bluff Drive-In . . . Absolutely *no one* will be admitted."

Fly Me

On a live network TV drama, the pretty young stewardess on the trans-Atlantic flight had just finished passing out a snack consisting of mixed drinks and assorted salted nuts, when the plane went into some turbulent air. In an effort to calm the passengers, she turned her microphone on and advised them, "We are temporarily experiencing some turbulence, but this should pass in a moment. In the meantime, please hold on to your glasses and nuts."

Knock on Wood

QUIZMASTER: Are you a vegetarian, sir?
CONTESTENT: Oh, no, I'm a carpenter.

Easy Does It!

When Johnny Carson had the sexy Golddiggers as guests on the Tonight Show, he asked who was the tallest, shortest, quietest, youngest. After getting replies from the girls on all those questions, Carson then asked, "And who's the easiest . . ." The audience broke up with laughter before he could complete his sentence, ". . . to get along with?"

Honest John

During coverage of "Operation Cactus," a seizure of several hundred pounds of marijuana at the Texas/Mexican border, John Chancellor read the following interesting material:

CHANCELLOR: There was a really big bust in Texas today, as U.S. and Mexican officials seized more than 500 pounds of marijuana as it was being carried across the border. This was the result of several months of investigation under the auspices of Operation Cactus, which has been described by both Mexican and American spokesmen as a *joint* effort.

Later Than You Think

Miami residents were puzzled when Lynn Russel, a WKAT radio personality, gave the time as "twenty-two minutes past 8:30."

Advance to the Rear

Charo, the vivacious wife of band leader Xavier Cugat, speaks only broken English. However, due to her bubbly personality, she is a favorite on talk shows. When she was introduced to Fernando Lamas on the Merv Griffin Show one afternoon, she shocked the audience, and the worldly Mr. Lamas, when she announced, "Oh, I know all about you . . . I looked up your behind!" As the audience and other guests rocked with laughter, they realized she meant she had looked up his past.

Udder Chaos

Perhaps the news teletype writer could have chosen different words for this story read by Sheila Young over BBC Radio in Bristol, England: "Due to a sudden outbreak of swine visicular disease, all cattle movements have been stopped."

So Long

We wonder if it was a blooper or a Freudian slip when an announcer, who was reading a promotional spot for an up-coming musical program, referred to the violinist (who shall remain nameless) as a *"violin virtuososo."*

Burned Bras

Joey Bishop told his late-night viewers the following: "I was really shocked today. I was on Fifth Avenue, and the Women's Libbers were marching two abreast."

Funny Girl

SPORTSCASTER: Alumnae flocked to the homecoming fes-
tivities, and enjoyed a hotly-contested football game, followed
by the clowning of the new homecoming queen, Mary Beth
Warren.

Homing Pigeon

When actor Walter Pidgeon appeared for a local bond drive, he was greeted by the president of the Drive, who was thrilled at the thought of meeting a movie star. The result of his excitement was the following: "Mr. Privilege, this is indeed a pigeon."

Occasional Pieces

A long-time announcer at WBAT radio in Marion, Indiana, fell victim to a copywriter's mistake, and came out with the following: "Reiger's furniture store features the finest, most durable furniture available. Shop at Reiger's, where we have been servicing the housewife for twenty-six years."

Call a Plumber

ANNOUNCER: Remember that bulk is important to the digestive track to aid in regular movement. Mother should have a good stock of Kellogg's Pep so that you can have a bowl every morning. Yes, kids, be sure Mother is *stopped* up with Kellogg's Pep."

A Sad Tail

Bud Collyer, popular radio and television master of ceremonies, relates the one about one of radio's best known news commentators. The newscaster hadn't gone over his news material in advance this particular evening. He was reading a news item about a prize-winning dog who had been crated and shipped from one city to another. It seemed that the valued dog got his tail caught in the crate. The tail apparently was removed, and the irate owner sued for $10,000 in damages. The commentator unhesitatingly said: "That's a lot of money for a piece of tail." There was a moment of silence while he mulled that one over.

Street Walkers

On the New Year's Eve Tonight Show, Johnny Carson was interviewing some girls who were working in a nightclub that happened to be on strike. The girls were unhappy about the strike, so Johnny asked, "Why aren't you girls out on the streets?" (AUDIENCE STARTS LAUGHING) . . . "What I really meant is, why aren't you picketing?"

Half Dozen of One, Six of the Other

Movie commercial: "Coming next week to the Strand Theatre, lovely Doris Day, starring in "With Sex You Get Eggroll . . . With *Six* You Get Eggroll!"

Pow!

"See the adventures of Bobin and Ratman this afternoon at 4:00 P.M. . . . Robin and Batman!"

Cleansing His Soul

People act strangely when they are near a microphone or a TV camera. A classic example is a porter who went into a BBC studio just after a live transmission. Seeing what he thought was a dead microphone, he walked up to it and declared, "This is the BBC, and this is William Robinson cleaning it." What Mr. Robinson did not know was that the microphone was "live" and that his profound statement was heard during the course of a religious church service broadcast to the nation.

He's Got to Go

Johnny Carson once said on the Tonight Show, "Here's how to relieve an upsex stomach . . . I mean an upset stomach . . . with Sex-Lax . . . Ex-Lax!"

Black is Beautiful

A WNAJ, Mississippi, newscaster got inadvertently mixed up when he read this item about a bank robbery: "Police say a bank in Holly Springs was robbed a few minutes ago. An eye-witness has identified the robber as about 5' 11" and wearing a black ladies' wig . . . uh, lady's black wig."

One on One

Curt Gowdy, reporting the NCAA Basketball finals, confused listeners with this: "Rex Morgan winds up his career today, the only starter in the starting line-up."

How Does That Grab You?

When Joan Rivers hosted the Tonight Show one evening, her guests were Hugh O'Brien and Marty Allen. The discussion was about groupies, and how they fight to get pieces of clothing and locks of hair from their favorite entertainers.
JOAN: Hugh, you're so good-looking . . . did any woman ever try to grab anything of yours?
HUGH: Uh, well . . . (AUDIENCE STARTS BREAKING UP)

JOAN: I mean clothing, silly.
ALLEN: That ain't all they grab!

Affairs of State

NEWSCASTER: Henry Kissinger, President Nixon's whorin' affairs advisor . . . *foreign* affairs advisor, today told newsmen about his latest lady friend.

Strange Weather

A weatherman reported, "A line of thunderstorms is moving steadily southweird."

Picture This

Public service messages are frequently read by laymen whose lack of professional training makes them very susceptible to on-the-air Bloopers. Here's an example that was broadcast over a small FM station in the northeast:

"The police department wants young, aggressive men to consider a life in law enforcement. New recruits are given intensive training in handling of firearms, marksmanship, self-defense and finger-painting."

Movies Are Better Than Ever

A female radio personality, who shall remain nameless, advised her listeners of the following: "I saw 'The Godfather' last night, and it was terrific! One of the most exciting films I have ever seen. If you get a chance, go see it, but don't bother buying refreshments . . . you'll never be able to watch popcorn and eat 'The Godfather' at the same time."

Freudian Slip

Heard on Johnny Carson's "Tonight Show":
ED MC MAHON: So stop in at your nearby hot pint dealer for a demonstration . . . I mean your near boy Hotpoint dealer!

From Dixie

Station break: "Stay tuned for a program of jazz, featuring the Dicks of Duxiland . . . I mean the Dukes of Dixieland!"

That's Rich!

When rookie outfielder Rich Chiles was interviewed for the first time on national television, he was understandably nervous. Sportscaster Loel Passe asked him how fast he could run, and got this surprising answer:

"Well, I've run from home plate to first base in under four seconds, which is pretty fast, but of my hits have been to the outfield, so I don't really have to bust my ass . . . that is, I don't really race to first base on hits to the outfield."

Punch Line

A sportscaster at WCAX-TV, Burlington, Vermont, was giving information about the fighting career of Mohammed Ali, when he came out with this delightful spoonerism: "Ali's next *fitle tight* will be held in a few months."

Under Cover Work

On the syndicated game show "Anything You Can Do," host Gene Wood told a contestant, "Now try to pull the blanket out from under you in one swell foop!" After the young lady had completed the stunt, Gene asked her, "Now, Amy, have you ever had so much fun on a blanket before?"

One Way to Score

Heard on KYTV, Springfield, Missouri: "And today, in the National League Pennant Rape . . . Race! . . . the Pissburgh Pirates are on top."

General Disappointment

The accidental deletion of the letter "s" in a news story caused an unsuspecting radio announcer to read the following news item: "The sagging morale of army nurses has been attributed to their dissatisfaction with military bras. I'm sorry, that should be *brass*."

Food for Thought

NEWSCASTER: And word has just reached us of the passing of Mrs. Angela Cirrillio, who died at the age of eighty-seven. Mrs. Cirrilio was a noted amateur chef who specialized in Italian cooking. There are no survivors.

Lordy!

On "The Newlywed Game," the announcer asked this question: "Who will your wife say was the first person to enter your house or apartment?" The husband's answer was "the landlord." When it was time for the wife to answer, she said, "It was my mother-in-law." The disappointed husband said, "I thought it was the landlord." "No, silly. That was before we were married!" said the determined spouse.

Double Meaning

Peter Lawford and Shelley Winters were discussing the selling price Lawford was asking for his beach house.

PETER: It's only a two-bedroom house, Shelley.
SHELLEY: Yes, but they're all so used looking as I remember them. (AUDIENCE STARTS TO LAUGH) . . . I didn't mean that!

Ain't It a Shame

Station announcement: "BBC presents William Shakespeare's 'The Shaming of the Trew' tonight at nine."

Having a Ball

A disc jockey on WHLO, Akron, Ohio, announcing the next record, came up with this Blooper: "And now, here's Gary Lewis and the Playballs . . . uh . . . that's Playboys!"

Wine, Women and Thong

Commercial: "Next time you are entertaining, be sure to have on hand Italian Swish . . . I mean Italian *Swiss* Colony Wine."

Consult Your TV Guide

"See 'Dragnet,' featuring actual criminal cases from the files of the Los Angeles Police Farce, starring Sergeant Thursday, on Friday . . . I mean Sergeant *Friday*, on Thursday."

Hi, Hun!

The quiz show question was: "Who was Kubla Kahn? The nervous contestant answered, "He was one of the mongrels who conquered China."

Bandaid Sheer Strip

KBFI-TV, Dallas, Texas, was the scene of a classic blooper, when a member of the six o'clock news team read the following: "A stripper was arrested today in Denton, Texas for wearing only two bandaids during her act. I sure hope they were ouchless." Unable to resist temptation, the anchor man then interjected, "I'm glad you're keeping abreast of the situation."

Wild Pitch!

After a Montreal Expos-Brooklyn Dodgers game, sportscaster Russ Taylor was advising listeners in Montreal about the rest of the major league baseball scores when he made this classic blooper:

". . . and Tom Seaver of the New York Mets pitched a two shit hutout . . . er, two hit *shutout* against the San Diego Padres."

Sic Religious

Years ago, Jack Gregson was a back up announcer for CBS radio. Finally, the time came for him to do his first coast-to-coast live broadcast, a religious program. He introduced a hymn as " 'The Lord Shall Lead His Shock of Fleep,' sung by the Mormon Tabernickle Choir."

Let's Make a Deal

No comment on this used car commercial from a TV station in Indiana:

"Friends and neighbors, we have such a wide selection of new and used cars that we want you to come down right now and make a deal. Bring your wife along and we can dicker."

You Can't Take It With You

In an on-the-air obituary on WVMG, Cochran, Georgia, the novice announcer read, ". . . survivors include two dollars . . . (BREAK UP) . . . that is *daughters*."

Loose Talk

DISC JOCKEY: Up next, a very popular song. Here's Andy Williams singing "Can't get Loose to Using You."

Budding Genius

Surprised North Dakota radio listeners were told about an exhibition by a millionaire art connoisseur who would be displaying "the newly-acquired bust of his twelve-year-old granddaughter on TV."

Bull's Eye!

NEWSCASTER: . . . when F.B.I. agents boarded the plane, a fight began. During the struggle, the hijacker's gun went off, wounding a stewardess in the tail section.

The Other Side of Barbra Streisand

"See Barbra Streisand portray Funny Brice in Fanny Girl."

Oh, Rats!

NEWS ANNOUNCER: The rioting hippies were finally brought under control after police sprayed mice into the crowd . . . excuse me, I think that should have been mace!

Cocktail Party

NEWSMAN: Political experts admit that Agnew originally rode into office on Nixon's cocktails, but insist that he will be elected on his own merit in 1976.

Improved Erection

A guest on a late radio show was discussing religious music, when he told the listeners, ". . . yes, well the acoustics of that cathedral have greatly improved since the building's erection in the late 1800's. Apparently much of the sound in those days was absorbed by the voluminous skirts of female parishioners, but nowadays, with the emergence of the mini-skirt, the old organ really goes to town."

Side Effects

While doing a radio play-by-play description of a Red Sox baseball game, Ned Martin made this comment about one opposing player: "Danny, as you know, was hospitalized last week after complaining about chest and sideburns."

Queer Statement

Des O'Connor, popular host of his own television program in England, finished a song, and then read the lead-in to a commercial as follows: "When I sit down to watch television with my husband . . ." A look of horrified amazement spread across his face.

Adults Say the Darnedest Things

When Art Linkletter interviewed Hedda Hopper on a TV program several years ago, he asked about a certain popular male star. The candid Hedda replied, "Oh, he's on his fifth wife now."

That's The Truth!

Bob Barker asked one of his contestants on "Truth or Consequences" what her hobbies were, and she told him she was very active in square dancing. Barker asked if that was all she was active in. The lady replied that she also had five children, and this caused Barker to respond as follows: "I'm sure you were quite active in that, too!"

Friendly Enemies

Merv Griffin, while competing with Johnny Carson for late night talk show ratings, came out with this Blooper: "Two weeks ago the TV Academy gave me a dinner just so they wouldn't have to give me an enemy . . . Emmy!"

Hot Stuff
Maybe the Colonel makes his chicken differently in Illinois, because an announcer in Waukegan told his listeners: "So rush right down to the Colonel's and have some Kentucky Fired Chicken!"

Busted
A D.J. at a top forty station, WRKO, made this apt comment about buxom Bobbie Gentry's latest record, "Now here's the big bust out of the bayou country . . . Miss Boobie Gentry! . . . uh, that's *Bobbie* Gentry."

Honkey Tonk
Johnny Most is the Boston Celtics' basketball radio play-by-play announcer, who occasionally does the sports reports for WHDH. On one particular show, he read the following: "And on the scoreboard in the National Honkey League . . ."

Misery Loves Company
Johnny Carson was doing a bit on the "Tonight Show" called "Misery is . . .", when one of the gags came out this way: "Misery is having the funny feeling that while you are undressing, a guy is looking at you through his bernockerlers! binockillers . . . a telescope!!"

Lust for Life
ANNOUNCER: Ladies, does your husband wake up in the morning feeling lustless . . . er, listless?

Color Him Yellow
Back in 1957, Mel Venter had a live radio program called "The Breakfast Gang," broadcast from San Francisco. He had a seven-year-old boy on as a guest one day, and he made the mistake of asking the boy, "Would you describe me to the radio audience?" After spending a few minutes telling the listeners about Venter's clothes, the little boy revealed to the audience that, "He has big ears." The laughter had almost died down from that one, when the boy came out with, "And he has yellow teeth."

No News Is Good News

The nation of Zambia has a growing broadcast industry, with many new announcers who have only recently learned to speak English. Our short-wave monitor picked up this classic Blooper:

NEWSCASTER: And now, here *are* the news."

Snow Job

WMEX Radio in Boston used to feature a Ski Report handled by Cousin Duffy, a staff announcer. One memorable afternoon, Cousin Duffy told his listeners: "If you ski in Massachusetts, you'll find excellent conditions in Connecticut."

Nudie

On KOA, Denver, a newscaster told his audience, "Rita Hayworth is now resting on a Nevada Nude Ranch."

Tricky Dick

A young woman on the Dick Cavett Show was discussing women's liberation with her host, when she said she felt sorry for the women who were trying so hard to change things, because they "don't have the same apparatus as men do." The audience broke up and Cavett tried to cover the error by saying, "She means they don't have the same tools." It was quite a while before things calmed down again.

What's Up, Doc?

Apparently the writer was responsible for a classic blooper that occurred on the Marcus Welby program on January 4, 1972. Dr. Welby demonstrated his keen medical perception during a conversation with his son-in-law. They discussed Welby's daughter's pregnancy, and the good doctor advised the son-in-law, "Well, at least you're over the hump."

Jet Stream

NEWSCASTER: Word has just reached us that the B.E.A. 'Go-slow' is ended with a settlement of the work-to-rule by pilots of the British Urine Peean Airways.

Foggy Notion

WEATHER FORECASTER: As I look out the window, I hesitate to say that it is raining, as the weather bureau doesn't call it that. They call it fog. This is to tell you that the fog is overflowing the sewers!

Nervous Wreck

News item: ". . . and after examining the wreckage of the two automobiles, police told reporters it was a miracle that none of the passengers suffered injuries or serious death."

Uplifting Music

A disc jockey at WSAI, Cincinnati, announced a song by Harper's Bazaar in the following manner: "We now hear the 59th Street Bridge Song by Harper's Brassiere!"

Anyone Can Play

On ABC's popular game show, "Password," host Allen Ludden told a surprised contestant, "Come on over and play with Michael Landon . . . (AUDIENCE LAUGHTER) . . . Well, you know what I mean!"

A Case of Booze

As the district attorney on "The Edge of Night" gave his opening statement to the jury in a murder trial, he looked at them very seriously and said, "I am going to be very careful and build this step case by case."

Blushing Bride

The Newlywed Game has been the scene of numerous Bloopers. One of the real classics occurred when a young husband was asked, "What have you done since your wedding that you thought was funny, but your wife didn't?" After thinking it over for a minute, the husband said his wife was afraid of spiders, and that he had put one in the shower one day. His wife went in the bathroom, screamed, and ran out naked. A few minutes later, when the wife was on stage and heard about the question, she turned to her husband and said, "That doesn't count . . . that was *before* we were married!" Her face turned red as the audience broke up. She said, "I hope my mother isn't watching."

Strictly Legit
On a pre-Christmas program, Johnny Carson told his "Tonight Show" viewers: ". . . and now I am going to read some letters from legitimate children . . . (AUDIENCE LAUGHTER) . . . c'mon now, you know what I mean!"

Out of This World
When astronaut Wally Shirra appeared as a guest for an interview on "Meet The Press," panelist Lawrence Spivak asked, "How does it feel to be in a state of wastelessness?"

Watch Your P's and Q's
Don Wardell on Radio Luxemburg's "Music In The Night" late show blooped: "And back from the news we come to 'Fever' from Leggy Pee . . . folks, Peggy Lee."

Double Jointed
George Jessel, star of "Here Come the Stars," told Steve Allen, who was a guest on the program, "You know . . . not too many people know this, but years ago I was the bat boy for the New York Joints . . . Giants!"

Star Player
SPORTSCASTER: And from here in the press box it appears that Bart Starr, the great Green Bay Packer quarterback, had the wind knocked out of him, for which we are most grateful.

Wild Plug
Joey once made this Blooper on "The Joey Bishop Show": "Shelley Winters can be seen wild in the streets . . . (LAUGHTER) . . . in the movie, I mean."

America First

When Mrs. Eleanor Roosevelt visited England during the war, Britons were interviewed for their reactions. Wynford Vaughan Thomas asked one interviewee on a street in London, "How do you think she will be received?" He replied, "With all the heartfelt fervor of a brother nation struggling for its survival." "Are you hoping to see her yourself?" "Alas, no, I understand that only the United States Forces in this country are going to have intercourse with her."

Open Door Policy

When Governor Rockefeller criticized Mayor Lindsay's handling of the New York City garbage strike, Lindsay wanted to broadcast a rebuttal. He assumed the speech was being taped for later broadcast, and did not know his words were going out over the air live when he said: "The city will, of course, endeavor in every way to remove the dangerous accumulation of trash from the sidewalks and streets. I will have a full report for the people in a news conference from City Hall tomorrow. (LOUD NOISE FROM BACKGROUND) We've got to do it again . . . the f---in' door was open."

Sticky Situation

Even the President of the United States can be the victim of a Blooper. In a nationally televised speech about the economy, Richard Nixon warned the public: "We are preaching a gospel of goo . . . er . . . glue . . . gloom!"

Ten Feet Tall

Sportscaster Bill Derne, broadcasting the Miami-Georgia Tech football game, blooped, ". . . and now coming into the game is the five-ton junior from Canton, Ohio."

No Time Like the Present
ANNOUNCER: At the chime it will be the correct time.

I Beg Your Pardon!
Chris Musk, disc jockey at MANX radio, Isle of Man, interviewed me in connection with my first Decca PARDON MY
BLOOPER record album release in England, for his "Summer
Sunshine" radio program. Chris had been vaguely familiar
with my American Blooper record albums and books. In the
spirit of politeness he blooped: "Kermit, I have always enjoyed your bloomers!"

Whoops!
The folowing was heard at the beginning of the Jet-Colt football game at the Super Bowl. A statistical comparison between
the two teams appeared on the screen. Commentator Curt
Gowdy said, "To give you a better idea of how the teams
shape up against each other, we'll be throwing up statistics
like these all during the game."

Good Timing
Station WKTY, La Crosse, Wisconsin, broadcasts a prayer at
noon each day. One day the tape of the prayer was started
too early, and when the announcer finally realized his mistake,
he simply shut it off and went on with his own announcements. The result was: "The angel of the Lord declared unto
Mary . . . the time is now 11:25."

Good Heavens!
Art Linkletter asked a little boy what was the best way to go
to heaven. The answer? "Die!"

New Dance Craze

Newscasters covering rocket launchings sometimes put in very
long hours, and, as a result, are not always as alert as they
should be. One such announcer was trying to fill in with talk
while waiting for a film to be shown, when he blooped: "In
just a moment we'll be showing you a film of the Moon
boogie . . . uh, that is Moon *buggy!*"

Screwed Up

On a radio discussion program, the host and his guest, a labor expert, were talking about factories and assembly lines. The conversation went like this:

HOST: They're finding out that the mass production line is causing too many rejects.

GUEST: Well, what I think it is, too, is the dullness.

HOST: That's right, and the other thing is that we've got a lot of young guys working in the automobile factories who don't dig this screw all day long . . . one screw, one screw, one screw.

GUEST: That's right.

HOST: And they're bored with the job, and any way they stick it in is okay.

I'm Just Wild About Harry

When Harry Belafonte was a guest on the Mike Douglas Show, he talked about his family and told Mike, "I have several children, the oldest twenty-four." Mike then asked Harry how long he had been married, to which Belafonte replied, "Seventeen years." As Mike began counting on his fingers, Belafonte said, "Hey, I've been married before!"

Let's Be Frank

DISC JOCKEY: And now we hear "It Was A Very Good Year" by the chairman of the broad, Frank Sinatra.

Marry the Girl!

The emcee of "The Newlywed Game" asked the husbands what one thing put down their male ego before they were married. One happy groom came up with, "When she said we would have to wait until we got married!"

Tonight's the Night

On the twelfth anniversary of the Tonight Show, Johnny Carson had a number of special guests, including his wife. The next night, as Johnny was doing his opening monologue, someone from the audience asked, "Is your wife here tonight?" Carson replied, "No, she only comes on anniversaries." The audience broke into good-natured laughter.

Pitch Man

A local announcer was doing the sports report for his radio station, when he Blooped the following: "Ted Williams is certain that his middle team will be hitting soon, but his main concern now is the men that his pishers . . . pissers . . . that is, pitchers, keep putting on base."

From Bed to Worse

A Virginia announcer was doing a radio promotion for a department store that had Chris Hanburger of the Washington Redskins available to sign autographs for fans. What the listeners heard was, "Stop by Leggett's to eat Chris Hanburger, Defensive Team Captain and Linebacker for the Washington Bedskins . . . MEET!"

A Bag of Wind

WEATHER FORECASTER: And the latest report from the United States Weather Bureau advises us that typhoid Ida is now threatening the Philippines! . . . typhoon Ida!

Thanks a Lot

Former Governor John Connally of Texas defended Spiro T. Agnew thusly. "Future events will prove him guilty . . . INNOCENT!"

All Wet

Don Dive, British Decca record album promotion man, tells about the disc jockey who played a recording by "The Living Strings," titled, "I Guess I'll Have To Hang My Tears Out To Dry." However, the radio audience heard this Blooper: "And now we spin another record . . . this time we hear The Living Strings playing, 'I Guess I'll Have To Hang My Dreams Out To Dry.'"

Good Ears

Back in the days when dramatic programs were produced live on radio, Bloopers were commonplace. For instance, one time the writers of the Lone Ranger Show were trying to indicate in the script that the townspeople, who were trapped in a cave, were about to be rescued by the famous masked man. Radio listeners heard one character, supposedly holed-up in the cave, deliver this immortal line: "Listen . . . I hear a white horse coming!"

Out of Sight

NBC-TV's John Chancellor told of a rash of recent UFO sightings. A woman who swore in a TV interview that she had seen unidentified flying objects, was asked how she could be so sure that they were, in fact, unidentified flying objects. She confidently replied, "They had the letters 'UFO' on the side."

Slice of Life

One of Johnny Carson's guests on the Tonight Show was an actor who spoke of his bad luck with women. He told Johnny he had invited a girl over for dinner and she stayed for three months. Then he added, "But she was a good cook." Johnny replied, "Three months! She must have made good bed . . . bread!"

Fly Us
NEWSMAN: The hijackers allowed all passengers to leave the plane safely, leaving only the pilot, co-pilot and a coo of troo screwardesses.

Bank Night

Open mikes can be treacherous. Here is a case where a listener phoned a disc jockey several times, inquiring if the banks were open on Veterans Day. In disgust, and believing his mike was not open, the disc jockey came out with . . . "If he is so concerned with the banks being open, why doesn't the son of a bitch call the banks himself!"

Odd-ities in the News

Heard on the NBC-TV Today program: "Since we have been on television, we have had fifty odd Senators and Representatives on our program!"

Screwed Up

Taped from WMAL, Washington: "President Nixon says that the model cities program is better than the *ineffuctive* urban renewal program."

Curt Remark

When Curt Gowdy was giving the play-by-play description of the second game of the 1973 World Series, he surprised baseball fans everywhere with this statement: "Willie Mays won't start today, because the Mets' regular outfielder, Rusty Slob, will be playing. Wait, that's Rusty *Staub!*"

Late Returns

WNBC-TV in New York City ran a spot during their 7:00 to 7:30 news show, which advised listeners to tune in later that night for results of the Democratic run-off between Beame and Badillo . . . a race which had taken place a month earlier.

What a Grouch!

A contestant on Groucho Marx's "You Bet Your Life" TV program indicated that he and his wife had sixteen children. Groucho asked, "Why do you have so many children?" The man replied, "Because I like my wife." After a pause and a particularly long drag on his ever-present cigar, Groucho said, "I like my cigar, too, but I take it out sometime!"

Face Saving Device

A sportscaster at WSBK-TV was covering a Boston Bruins Hockey game when he came out with the following: "Here's Hodge on a breakaway! He's all by himself . . . he shoots . . . and Hodge missed the goal!! He'll be thinking about that one for a while. Just look at the expression on Hodge's stick!"

No News Is Good News

Radio station KTAC, Washington, was the site of an unusual newscast. The regular newscast music finished up, and the announcer came in with, "And now the news at this hour . . . (LONG PAUSE) . . . Where the hell's the news? . . . Christ, where's the news?" For the next sixty seconds, listeners heard only the sound of the announcer laughing.

Hair Apparent

Bloopers are not just limited to American radio and TV stations, as Channel 7 in New Brunswick, Canada found out. A dandruff commercial was not quite finished, when a second commercial cut in with:

"Risdan was made to control dandruff, and does control dandruff. How can you improve on that? . . ."
". . . (CUT IN WITH CARMELITA POPE) . . . Spray it with Pam! Also good for frying pans."

He's Just Going Through a Phase

The anchor man on KABC, California's Eyewitness News program, told his surprised listeners: "Today President Eisenhower announced Phase Four . . . oh . . . I mean Mr. Nixon announced freeze four!"

Grapes of Rath

Merv Griffin, host of his own popular talk-show, was describing a famous movie star on his program, but could not recall the man's name. He was getting more and more frustrated with himself, then suddenly he remembered the celebrity's name, and blurted out, "Rasil Bathbone!"

I'll Drink to That

An Illinois announcer who had had one too many before he went on the air with his regular sports and weather show, committed a classic Blooper. After tripping over a cable, he sat down in front of the camera and reported: "The game between the Chicago Cubs and the St. Louis Cardinals was rained out because of rain. The forecast for tomorrow's game will be mostly light with a few scattered sours."

New Wrinkle

"Gambit," a popular CBS game show, offers many prizes to it's contestants. One morning, the announcer was describing a sewing machine that was to be given away, when he informed the audience that it "never needs ironing . . . of course, I mean oiling."

Playing with Themselves

SPORTSCASTER: And now stay tuned for the wrap-up of the hookey game just played between the Rangers and the New York Rangers.

Baby Talk
Prescott Robinson of Channel 4 TV in Miami, Florida, gave the youth movement unexpected support when he read this news item: "Illinois is one of the last remaining states to approve voting rights for eight-year-olds."

That Sinking Sensation

A San Jose, California TV station had scheduled the movie "Up Periscope" to begin right after the 5:30 newscast. Perhaps the announcer was a former navy man, because, as the news ended, viewers heard him say, "Stay tuned for the six o'clock movie, 'Up Your Periscope!'"

An Athletic Supporter

There's a club for jockeys in Los Angeles, called the "Jock Trap." The day after one of the KMPC's announcers had interviewed jockeys at the club, he went on the air and told his listeners about the great interviews he had gotten at the "Jock Strap."

Here, Here!

In America, the word "boobs" has an entirely different meaning than it does in England. "Boobs" are commonly referred to as female breasts. In England, the word is synomymous with broadcasting fluffs. Imagine my consternation when I visited BBC Radio One in London for an interview and spoke with BBC commentator, Marion White, who volunteered the information that she had some "lovely boobs" to tell me about.

Air Time

When Gene Klavan was a young disc jockey, he was half of the team "Klavan and Finch" on WNEW in New York. One morning, while Gene was reading a commercial for a clothing store that was featuring windbreakers, he ad-libbed, "These jackets are guaranteed to break any wind." His partner, Finch, started giggling loudly, and Klavan still not realizing what he had said, made matters worse by insisting, "What are you laughing at?"

It Only Seems Like That
ANNOUNCER: This year, the government is issuing new forms for your Eternal Revenue Tax . . . uh . . . that's *Internal!*

Screwed Up
Sailors know that the word "screw" refers to the propeller part of a boat engine. Apparently the word threw the announcer for the game show, "Concentration," Hugh Downs, as he described one of the prizes, a beautiful motor boat. He was supposed to say "the motor has twin screws for pleasure cruising and fishing." What came out, however, was: "the motor has twin screws for pleasure screwing and fishing."

Tricky Dick
An NBC Special News Report informed the public that, "President Nixon has been hospitalized for a virile ailment . . . uh, *virule* pneumonia."

Super Fruit
Many listeners of WMAQ in Chicago were not aware that the announcer was leading into a Nectarine commercial, and were surprised to hear him say: "It won't be long before one of California's finest fruits disappears from your supermarket . . . (GIGGLES) . . . Of course I don't mean that kind of fruit . . . I'm talking about fruit fruit!"

The Duce to Pay
Norman Rosenman, who has been around broadcasting for a numbers of years, reports overhearing this unusual movie promo: "Stay tuned for the movie of the week, Irma La Douche."

Fairy Nice Program
STATION BREAK: "Stay tuned for the Word Quiz Show, sponsored by your local Dairmont Fairy . . . I mean, Fairmont Dairy!!!"

Prevents Accidents
ANNOUNCER: This special network presentation on abortion is brought to you by Goodyear Rubbers . . . Goodyear Rubber Tires!

Put Up Your Dukes
When the Duke of Bedford appeared on Merv Griffin's popular talk-show, he told a humorous story about several of the bedrooms in his mansion, while keeping quite a straight face. After he had finished, Merv commented, "How can you tell a funny story like that with such a bed-pan expression?" The audience broke up.

This Is a Raid!
Heard on WCBS Radio news in New York City: "Other stories in the news . . . Raiders Naders . . . oh God! . . . it should be *Nader's Raiders,* turned their attention to beat selts in automobiles."

Atsa Right
When Nipsy Russell was a guest on the popular game show "$10,000 Pyramid," he had to give clues to contestants about secret words or phrases. One of these phrases was "Tin Pan Alley," so Nipsy gave the clue, "The place where all songs are written." The audience broke into laughter when the nervous contestant replied: "Italy."

The Blooper Spirit

A network newsman read the following item about Howard Hughes:

ANNOUNCER: It appears that mystery man Howard Hughes has landed in England and has gone into hiding at the Inn-On-The-Park Hotel. Reporters were told that the aging millionaire would have to appear personally to renew his passport if he chose to stay in London, but no other information was forthcoming from the Hughes spooksman.

Shorts Subject

Perhaps the copywriter could have used better phrasing when he wrote this story and handed it to the unsuspecting announcer:

"Female employees of the firm went on strike today, alleging that the company is ultraconservative and will not tolerate the wearing of hot pants by its employees. The women also stated that anyone wearing hot pants to work must take them off or face immediate dismissal."

Undercover Man

Wilson Hatcher of Channel 41, Louisville, Kentucky, read the following movie promo: "Be sure to see 'Pretty Maids All In A Row,' headed by Rock Hudson and directed by Roger Vadim, the man who uncovered Brigitte Bardot and Jane Fonda."

Lover Boy

When a South Carolina disc jockey advised his listeners about who was up for Oscar nominations, he surprised them with this unintentional fluff: "And Richard Castellano received a nomination for best supporting actor for his performance in 'Livers and Other Strangers.' "

C'mon Down

The exclusive hotel which bought air time on a yankee radio station was trying to lure cold northerners down into the Florida sun. But they probably didn't get too many takers when a New Jersey announcer blooped the following: "The elegant penthouse of this luxurious, twenty-seven story resort hotel provides an expensive view of the Miami Beach waterfront . . . *expansive!*"

What's Cookin'?

Listeners in Lafayette, Indiana were shook up when the local station ran two commercials back-to-back, with this unappetizing result:

". . . What are you going to get from Burger Chef? What are you going to get, today?"

". . . pimples, blackheads, and acne are problems that plague teenagers everywhere."

It Never Fails

When a Chicago news announcer blew his lines several times on the air, he slammed down his copy and yelled "Goddamnit!!" The panicky director blacked out the regular picture, and put up a slide that said, "Please stand by, Network failure."

Something Not Kosher Here

NEWS ANNOUNCER: The victim of the dog attack, a four-year-old girl, was rushed to the hospital where doctors began the series of shots that will protect her from rabbis . . . uh, that is, rabies.

A Pregnant Thought

A University of Iowa student announcer learned how much damage a copywriter can cause, when he read the following public service announcement on the campus station:
". . . and all U. of Iowa students are invited to attend there will be, er . . . invited to attend. (PAUSE) There will be volleyballswimming, that is, volleyball *and* swimming, softball-badminton, and two live rock bands plus a lot more fun for you and your friends. Boy, the copywriter sure muffed this one, huh? Let's see, she left out one . . . two . . . three . . . four commas, and she missed a period, too!"

Middle East Conflict
Heard in Dallas, Texas: "A peculiarity of the young militants in this Arab/Israeli conflict, is the frequency of their emertional outboasts . . . emotional outboats!"

Oh Lord!
Jackson Harrell of KLWT, Lebanon, Missouri, inadvertently introduced a guest on a religious program in the following manner: "And now, here's the Reverend Bill Christ from the Church of Van Stavern."

Tough Weather
Weather forecaster on WRFM: ". . . we can expect some gutsy winds this evening."

Doing the Breast Stroke
After a commercial during a movie on Chanel 7 in Chicago, the announcer said, "And now we return to Jane Russell under water . . . I beg your pardon, I meant Jane Russell in 'Under Water.' "

The Eyes of Texas Are Upon You
Station break: "This is KTIW, Sexas Titty . . . er Texas City."

Everything Half Off
The Quick Trip grocery store advertises on KTUL, Tulsa, Oklahoma. Unfortunately, one of the announcers read a live piece of copy that came out this way: "This portion of the news is brought to you by Quick Strip grocery store, where we can service your every need."

Here Comes the Bride

Richard Whitely, an announcer on England's Yorkshire Television show "Calendar," was doing a special program celebrating the Queen's silver wedding anniversary. He interviewed a young couple who had come straight from their registry office wedding to the studio. When he asked the blushing bride what it was like to be married, she unblushingly replied, "I can't say . . . it hasn't sunk in properly yet."

Frug It!

Tom Adams of WIOD in Miami, Florida, reported this classic boner made by a fellow announcer: "The recalling of several thousand cans of mushrooms believed to be infected with botulism, was ordered today by the Dude and Frug Administration."

He's Not the Type

SPORTSCASTER: And in the Eastern Playoffs of the NBA tonight, it was Philadelphia 122, Cincinnati 114, with Cincinnati winning that one . . . (OFF MIKE) . . . I'll be goddamned . . . now how the hell is that possible! . . . Hey, Charlie . . . who the hell typed this?

Take Your Choice

Curt Gowdy, broadcasting a play-by-play account of the All Star Baseball game, gave listeners the final score: "And at the game's end, it's National League Six, American League Four. That score again is American League Six and National League Four."

Out to Launch

NEWSCASTER: And a disappointed nation heard the glum news that the United States has suffered another setback in the space race. It is becoming quite apparent that our country is more and more gaining a reputation for its space failures rather than for its accomplishments. No further announcements pertaining to any new rocket launch attempts are expected from rocketeers at Cape Carnival for some time . . . I mean Cape Canaveral.

It's a Corker
Commercial: "So, for those who think young, be sure you're stacked up with a Pepsi Sex pack . . . stopped up . . . stocked up with a Pipsi six pack."

One Too Many
STATION BREAK: "It is now nine P.M., Eastern Standard Time . . . On behalf of all of the personnel here at this station, we want to wish all our viewers season's greetings and a very happy and preposterous new year . . . hic!"

The Price Is Right
Political speech: "And if I'm elected, I can promise you the finest local government that money can buy!"

Who's on First
A TV station in Lufkin, Texas, went off the air for several hours because of transmission difficulties. A hand bearing this hastily-scrawled message appeared on viewers' screens: "We have temporarily lost our slide informing you that we have temporarily lost our picture. Please bear with us!"

Horsing Around
Every British commentator dreads state occasions featuring the Royal Horse Artillery. More than one has described them as "the Queen's Troop of The Royal Arse Hortillery."

Ballin' the Jack
From Jack de Manio's book "To Auntie with Love" comes this gem. Two young ragamuffins had strayed into the BBC's Overseas premises at Bush House in the Strand. No one knows how they got there, or what they thought they were doing. All that was ultimately known was that while the news reader was holding forth to the rest of the world these two urchins, having decided to take a left turn rather than a right, burst into the news studio, crept up behind the news reader and shouted, "BALLS TO THE BBC!" They then vanished out the door.

House of Ill Repute
NEWS ANNOUNCER: The trial of the two prostitutes continues tomorrow at the Corny County Cathouse . . . uh, that is the Cory County Courthouse!

From Out of the Blue
On a dreary, overcast day, a weather forecaster in Washington blooped the following: "And this evening, we will have some miserable precipitation . . . uh, that should be *measurable* prepisitation!"

Hair Raising Blooper
On the afternoon soap opera, "As The World Turns," which was live, one of the actors was having an emotional confrontation with his TV "daughter," when his toupee slowly slid right off his head, unbeknownst to the poor fellow!"

Lost His Head
Overheard during the broadcast of a Miami Dolphins pro football conference game: "Paul Warfield ran a beautiful post pattern, putting his body between himself and the defenders."

Take It Off!
Educational TV: "And now, class, we come to the moment you have all been waiting for . . . a strip film . . . oops . . . I mean a film strip on farming!"

Making Ends Meat
Larry Blyden, hosting *What's My Line*, had two young girls as his next contestants. Blyden gave the customary hint to the panelists, by telling them that the girls "work after school and on work ends."

Whistle While You Work
A disc jockey announced the popular song "Sing you Sinners" thusly: "And now, here's some great musical advice to all you listeners . . . Sin You Singers."

Out of This World
An announcer at KVI, Seattle, Washington, surprised his listeners with this news item: ". . . and the soviet spice satellite has gone into orth erbit . . . er . . . earth orbit.

Under the Weather
WEATHER FORECASTER: This is your KBEL, Oklahoma, weatherman . . . currently under partly cloudy skies . . . with a temperature of seventy-four degrees Fahrenheit and sixty-three degrees centipede.

A Bad Spell of Weather
Rick Jeffries of KTKT, Tucson, Arizona, gave his listeners this welcome bit of weather information: ". . . little change in rain, and no chance of temperature."

A Little Bit Pregnant
It isn't easy to turn out a live half-hour soap opera five days a week, especially for the actors and writers. Understandably, not all script errors are caught before air-time. For an example, here's one that happened on General Hospital, one of the most popular of the detergent dramas:

ACTRESS: It's just that I think that he's thinking about Jessie, since they're technically married most of the time.

Ups and Downs
A New Hampshire announcer's mind was obviously not on his work when he gave the daily stock market report which included the following information: "After a fast increase this morning, Wall Street storks dropped nine pints on the Dow-Jones averages."

Hits, Runs and Errors

A Boston Red Sox announcer made this blooper during a game between the Sox and the Cleveland Indians: "And here's Cleveland's Chris Chambliss. Chambliss has 14 home runs and 3 runs batted in . . . uh, thats 3 home runs and 14 runs batted in! . . . that other would be a little hard to do, wouldn't it? . . . (OFF MIKE) . . . Where the hell did we get these stastiffcates?"

Wanted Dead or Alive

NEWSCASTER: "Officials are still trying to locate two miners who are trapped in the mine shaft. They don't know if the men are still dead, or if they are alive. . . . (OFF MIKE) . . . The news department sure gave *me* the shaft on this one!"

What a Gas!

A newscaster on WWCH, Clarion, Pennsylvania, gave his listeners quite a shock when he read the following news story: "Yesterday, 7000 peasants suffering from encephalitis, a type of sleeping sickness, were gassed to death in New Hampshire . . . that should be *pheasants!*"

Who's Fooling Who?

On a local news program, a little girl was being interviewed about her father, who was serving in Vietnam at the time. The conversation went like this:

GIRL: Daddy always used to fool around and call me his only girl.
ANNOUNCER: What did your Mommy say about that?
GIRL: Nothing. She used to fool around, too.

They're Not Bored

In a news story carried on Channel 4 TV in Miami, the following was heard: "In addition to their small salaries, the migrant workers are usually given bread and broad . . . uh, that is bed and board."

I'll Drink to That!

When one of England's Members of Parliament decided not to run for re-election, television cameras were on the scene for his unforgettable statement: "Having *swerved* in the House of Commons for nearly two decades, I feel it time to step down."

Something Not Kosher Here
Commercial: "Remember, for this week only, Food Fair is featuring a Passover special on Rath bacon and ham."

Honest John
When "Those Magnificent Men in Their Jaunty Jalopies" played on a Georgia TV station, a commercial cut in when Tony Curtis was proposing to his girl friend. What listeners heard, was: "And if I win the race, I will find you, get down on one knee, and say . . . (CUT IN) . . . Does your toilet bowl need cleaning?"

Truer Words Were Never Spoken
Garry Moore, host of the popular "To Tell The Truth" show, introduced a commercial this way: "Now we pause for an outrageous commercial . . . uh . . . a courageous commercial . . . sorry."

Holy Mackerel!!!
When I returned from London, after several appearances on BBC television and radio in connection with the release of my books and record albums throughout England, I was greeted at the airport by April Kelly, my girl friday, who told me that she had some perplexing news. The post office had contacted our office to advise us that they had received a stack of books which we were to pick up. This mysterious shipment came at a time when my previous book, Best of Bloopers, had just been released by Avenel Books. We headed directly to the post office from the airport. Upon opening one of the packages, we saw the "Best of Bloopers" covers. April opened one of them up, only to find that the bindery had made an error. Within the Blooper covers were Bible dictionaries! We were witness to the strangest Blooper of all!